YOU'RE HIRED!
JOB HUNTING ONLINE
THE COMPLETE GUIDE

YOU'RE HIRED! GUIDES

See our website at www.trotman.co.uk for a comprehensive list of published and forthcoming Trotman titles.

YOU'RE HIRED!
JOB HUNTING ONLINE
THE COMPLETE GUIDE

TRISTRAM HOOLEY, JIM BRIGHT, DAVID WINTER

You're Hired! Job Hunting Online: The complete guide

This first edition published in 2016 by Trotman Publishing, a division of Crimson Publishing Ltd, 19–21c Charles Street, Bath BA1 1HX

© Trotman Publishing 2016

Authors Tristram Hooley, Jim Bright, David Winter

British Library Cataloguing in Publication Data
A catalogue record for this book is available from the British Library

ISBN 978 1 84455 628 1

Please note that all websites given in this book are subject to change so you may find that some of these sites in time may be renamed, merge with other sites or disappear.

Designed by Nicki Averill
Typeset by IDSUK (DataConnection) Ltd
Printed and bound in the UK by Ashford Colour Press, Gosport, Hants

CONTENTS

ABOUT THE AUTHORS

The authors met online. After a series of intense debates, the swapping of jokes, information and gossip they met in a pub in London. Somewhere along the lines a plan was hatched to write a book about the internet and careers. This is that book. Its very creation demonstrates that the internet can help us to learn, develop our careers and find new ways of working with people all over the world.

Tristram Hooley is Professor of Career Development at the University of Derby. He writes, researches and thinks about career and career development all the time. He is particularly interested in the intersection between careers, politics, technology, research and appearance. He is an enthusiastic user of the internet for both work and play. Tristram can be found on Twitter at @pigironjoe, via his blog Adventures in Career Development (www.adventuresincareerdevelopment.wordpress.com) and on a whole host of other social media sites if you search hard enough.

Jim Bright is Professor of Career Education and Development at the Australian Catholic University. He is also Visiting Professor of Career Development at the University of Derby. In addition he runs a Career Management Consultancy, Bright and Associates, and writes a weekly column on careers in the *Sydney Morning Herald*. Jim has written 12 books including the bestselling, *How to write a Brilliant CV* (Pearson). He is the co-author of the *Chaos Theory of Careers*. He is interested in complexity-based approaches to careers, evidenced-based careers advice, leadership and entrepreneurialism. He can be found on Twitter at @DrJimBright and is the owner of the Careers Debate Linkedin Group. He has developed careers tests related to luck, opportunity awareness and change perception (www.jimbright.com/tests).

David Winter is the Head of Consultancy and Research at The Careers Group, University of London, which provides coaching and training to support career, professional and leadership development in organisations. He co-led the world's first massive open online course (MOOC) on careers and employability, attracting over 130,000 participants from around the world so far. For several years he authored the blog Careers – in Theory (www.careersintheory.wordpress.com), looking at the impact of theory and research on careers practice. Now he focuses more on writing about leadership and communication (blog. thecareersgroup.co.uk/learning-and-professional-development-training/all). David can be found on Twitter as @davidawinter. He is interested in way too many things for his own good.

ACKNOWLEDGEMENTS

The authors would like to acknowledge the support of our friends, families and colleagues in the creation of this book. In particular we'd like to thank both Korin Grant and Susanna Winter for their constant support and indispensable feedback.

We would also like to thank Della Oliver for being an ever helpful and patient publisher.

WHO IS THIS BOOK FOR?

This book is for anyone who wants a little help in getting their career moving forwards. In particular, it is for people who are sure that they could be making more use of the internet in their career, but aren't sure where to start. It will also be useful for experienced internet users who want to check that they are doing everything right.

You don't have to be a technical wizard to get something out of this book. In fact the technophobes and internet newbies should get the most out of it. However, it isn't designed for people who have never used a computer or the internet before. If that is you, there are plenty of other books that you could go off and try. You will probably find it easier than you thought and will be able to graduate back to this book in a few weeks.

The book is aimed at people who are either currently in the workforce or who are about to come to the end of their studies. We believe that everyone could benefit from thinking a bit more about their career and in being given some tips about how best to move forward.

We hope that you find it useful.

A NOTE ON THE USE OF EXAMPLES AND URLS

This is a book about using the internet for your career. Inside you will find hundreds of suggestions of websites to look at that might support you in your career-building. The book is not a directory of websites but it is packed with the most helpful sites for building a career using social media! We set out the principles for getting the best out of any social media or careers website. The particular tools available online will change every day but the process of career-building changes much more slowly. We hope you find the examples we use useful.

We will introduce you to some excellent websites that can play a key role in enhancing your career. We offer example sites, but remember in this crazy online world, websites come and websites go – our selections will give you a great start, but over time you will find other great sites. The sites that we mention were all available at the time we went to press. In two years' time some of them will have changed. Thankfully, the practice of redirecting people to similar or alternative sites is growing on the internet.

INTRODUCTION: USING THE INTERNET TO ADVANCE YOUR CAREER

The internet is everywhere in our lives. We check websites to tell us what the weather is going to be, store our calendars on Outlook or Google Calendar and make arrangements with friends and colleagues through email and text. Tools such as Facebook help us to organise our social lives and keep in touch with our networks, others help us find a life partner or a holiday. We shop, consume information, watch media and play games online.

Increasingly, we access the internet not only on computers but through phones, tablets, watches and a host of other devices. The internet is always with us and it takes a conscious effort for us to disconnect and '*go dark*' for a week's holiday (and even then we might ensure our accommodation has wireless, just in case). This connected world can be exciting and empowering, but it can also be stressful and difficult. Making the most of it and managing its challenges is an increasingly important skill.

The internet has transformed how we live, communicate, shop and, increasingly, how we work and find work. The internet opens up opportunities for us to find work and find out about work, it allows us to build and sustain professional networks and to build our reputations, but there are also pitfalls that we need to avoid.

Of course, it is easy to get carried away by the impact of the internet. In many ways, the things you need to do in order to have a successful career have not changed at all. You still need to make good decisions based on the best information available. You still need to be alert to the appearance of appropriate opportunities. You still need to be able to build your reputation and your professional network. And you still need to be able to present your most winning qualities to prospective recruiters. The internet hasn't changed any of those things, nor has it entirely replaced the need to engage in more traditional offline job-hunting activities. However, it has opened up opportunities to do those things in potentially more efficient ways and on a larger scale.

This book will help you to make the most of the internet for your career. It will provide you with advice, tips and examples that will support you to use the internet to explore your career, build your reputation and employability, and move into the kind of jobs that you are interested in.

CASE STUDY

Consider the case of two aspiring executives: Diana and Joe. Both of them are fed up with their current jobs and are keen to move on and up.

Diana enthusiastically opens Google and starts researching the jobs that she is interested in. She identifies a number of sites that have jobs in her field and subscribes to them. She starts reading career advice blogs and chooses a few that she feels are trustworthy and reliable. She quickly builds her knowledge about what jobs are out there and what she might need to do to get one. Joe sticks to more conventional methods, waiting to hear about promotion opportunities in his company and looking for job adverts in the newspaper.

Diana joins LinkedIn and sets up an online profile explaining her skills and experience. She also uses the site to reconnect with a few old colleagues and joins some discussion groups relevant to her industry. She posts questions and comments to these groups and hopes that she is seen as a useful member of her professional community. She listens more than she talks on LinkedIn and gains some good insights into the latest trends in her industry. Meanwhile, Joe heads off for his professional association's annual conference. He learns a lot and comes back with a stack of business cards. He thinks: 'It would be nice if I could do this more often'.

Diana decides to Google herself to find out how she comes across online. She's disappointed. Apart from her LinkedIn profile there isn't very much about her at all online. She decides to start a blog and to write about the latest trends in her industry. She is nervous about setting it up but starts to post once a week. At first no one is watching, but she carries on anyway as it helps to focus her thinking about her industry. After about three months one of her blogs gets posted on Twitter and she gets 50 views in one day. People start to subscribe and she gradually builds up a small but professionally relevant following. When she Googles herself again after a year she finds loads of posts from her blog all talking about her professional interests. Joe never Googles himself, but if he did he would realise that the only digital footprint he has is a couple of photos from an event he attended last year (which he doesn't even know are online and doesn't remember attending) and the fact that he came fourth in the Greater Fulchester Fun Run in 1999.

The examples of Diana and Joe highlight the importance of the internet to your career. Joe isn't really doing anything wrong; he just isn't doing anything very much at all. In contrast, Diana is actively building her skills and her career and signalling to her professional world what she has to offer. At the end of a year she finds herself much more employable than Joe and easily moves into a better job.

Why does everyone keep talking about 'social media'?

'Social media' is one of those buzz phrases that everyone is using but no one ever takes the time to define. You've probably worked out that people often use it to describe online communication tools such as Facebook and Twitter, but if you haven't used those sites that probably isn't much help!

The term 'social media' is used to describe a very wide range of tools that allow individuals to communicate, share information and publish text, images, audio and video so that others can find it on the internet. LinkedIn, Pinterest, Tumblr and YouTube are all types of social media, and more strangely spelt names seem to be released every day.

There is no reason why you should try all of them, but we think that it will be useful for your career to try a few. We'll talk you through some of the most useful ones in this book and give you some tips about how to use them effectively.

Ten reasons why you should start using social media tools for your career

1.   To stay up to date with the latest news and views.
2.   To spot career opportunities.
3.   To find out what people are saying about you online.
4.   To build your reputation and tell the world that you exist.
5.   To meet new business contacts.
6.   To keep in touch with existing contacts more easily.
7.   To provide evidence to employers that you have digital skills.
8.   To showcase your best work.
9.   Because it is free.
10. Because it is much easier than you think.

About this book

This book will provide you with some practical advice about how to use the internet to advance your career. It is based on the following seven principles (each of which we devote a chapter to).[i]

1. **Change is inevitable – be an adventurous explorer.** The internet is changing the way that careers work. You need to embrace this change if you want to be successful in your career.
2. **Information is power – collect as much as you can.** Information about jobs and opportunities is out there on the internet, but you need to be good at looking for it.
3. **The internet is a jungle – be a critical thinker.** With so much information out there, you can't rely on all of it to be accurate and up to date. You need to develop the skills to critically evaluate the information you find.
4. **Networks are vital – be an effective connector.** You can use the internet to build a powerful professional network that will support your career-building.
5. **Interaction is important – be a perceptive communicator.** The internet is all about communication, but the most effective way to communicate will

depend on what you want to achieve and the nature of the tools you are using. Make sure your communication is honed to perfection.

6. **Building a brand – be a skilled storyteller.** The internet allows us to publish content about ourselves and our interests and to make that available to the world. You can make this work for your career.

7. **Your footprint lingers – be a diligent curator.** Most of us have created some kind of digital footprint. You should know what information about you exists online and think about the kind of impression you are making (remember, no information makes an impression too).

You don't have to read this book cover to cover. It is very likely that you will know some of this already, so feel free to pick and choose chapters you wish to focus on. However, you might be surprised by some of the chapters and find that there is a bit more to something you thought was simple (e.g. searching Google). For this reason, we start each chapter with a checklist of what it covers so you can quickly review it and decide where to focus your time.

In Chapter 1 we look at dealing with change. The internet has increased the speed of change in our lives and careers. If we are going to be effective we need to think about how to keep up. The chapter will explore making and remaking career plans; being positive about change; learning to adapt; and learning to use new software, web services and tools.

In Chapter 2 we cover how best to research jobs and careers options. It argues that information is critical for effective career-building and suggests that you should invest time and energy in increasing the information available. It sets out three approaches to accessing information: searching (finding what you are looking for); alerts (finding things even when you aren't looking for them); and networks (getting other people to find things for you). It also discusses strategies to avoid information overload.

In Chapter 3 we outline a number of ways in which information you find online might turn out to be unreliable or unhelpful. We will equip you with a range of tools and helpful habits to increase your chances of sorting the good from the bad. And the great thing is, many of these tools don't just apply to online information – you can use them to evaluate information you get from your Uncle Bernard's best friend's brother as well.

In Chapter 4 we will look at networks and networking online. Networking is really important for your career. The internet can help to increase your network and make better use of the contacts that you have. We'll help you to think about how best to network online, how to combine online networking with face-to-face networking, and to think about the tools that you need to be effective. We'll answer your questions about when to tweet and who to network with (and who to avoid).

In Chapter 5 we will help you to think about the career-related communication goals you can achieve online. We will give you practical tips for quickly learning the ground rules of any new social media environment and a number of practical communication tips for getting attention, engaging in interaction and creating good impressions. We will also discuss the best ways to deal with some of the more troublesome inhabitants of the internet.

In Chapter 6 we'll show you how to build your personal brand in a way that makes you more likely to get offered great opportunities. To be effective you'll have to become a skilled storyteller, able to use blogs, videos and pictures to create a career image that is appealing to employers. We'll help you set up (or polish) your LinkedIn profile, start blogging and think about how to shape the messages that are out there about you.

In Chapter 7 we cover how to manage your online brand. How do you deal with what others are saying about you? What can you do about images that you've posted that you wish you hadn't? In general, we'll tell you how to make sure that your online profile is good and help you to hide the bad and the ugly stuff that is out there.

Finally, the book concludes with some thoughts about how you can draw all of this together and make the most of your career.

At the end of the book you will also find an internet-to-English dictionary which you can use to help understand the jargon that people throw at you.

1 CHANGE IS INEVITABLE – BE AN ADVENTUROUS EXPLORER!

Change is inevitable, except from a vending machine.

Our working lives are always changing. As the internet becomes an increasingly central part of work, it speeds up these changes.

In this chapter we share with you some tips about how to change your career plans, and changing your approach to make the most of this ever-changing world. We advise you to embrace the fast-moving reality of online careers and to keep on top of the (sometimes) bewildering changes happening within social media. If you are particularly interested in how change influences our careers, and want to read more deeply about this, you may wish to have a look at the book *The Chaos Theory of Careers* by Robert Pryor and Jim Bright.[ii]

This chapter will cover:

- making and remaking career plans

- being positive about change

- learning to adapt

- using new software and tools

- finding the time for social media.

Shift happens!

It is a reality of modern working life that shift happens. Change is occurring everywhere, driven by technological and scientific advances, changing tastes and expectations, political decisions and pressures, economic booms and busts.

In a few short decades from the 1970s and '80s we have gone from the aerogram (air letter) being the primary way to communicate with people in far-off lands to emails, instant messages, Skype and tweets. In between, we had the fax, the technological equivalent of the boy band – been, gone and forgotten.

Speeded up communication, and the mind-boggling possibilities for new interconnections between people, companies and nations, has led to sudden and unpredictable outcomes. When things get very connected, unpredictable things happen. Think about a Rubik's cube, the three-dimensional colour block puzzle. Have you ever tried to get one side of the cube all the same colour, only to find in doing so you have messed up another side you had previously worked on? The Rubik's cube only has 54 little coloured tiles, but because they are connected to each other, it turns out that there are 43 quintillion combinations of the cube! And the Rubik's cube is simple compared with the interconnections on the internet!

Image created by Booyabazooka and reproduced under a Creative Commons Attribution-Share Alike 3.0 Unported license (https://creativecommons.org/licenses/by-sa13.01).

What has this got to do with career plans? This highly connected world is one in which change happens quickly, unpredictably and sometimes dramatically. This means we need to be prepared to change our career plans. We have to be prepared to weather unexpected turbulence on the way to our goals. Setting goals is fine, but don't be surprised if the goal posts keep moving. If your goal in 2005 was to invest a lot in a marketing strategy for what was then the most popular social media site, MySpace, within three years you would have seen MySpace surpassed by Facebook. If you'd decided to buy MySpace in 2005 it would have set you back £378 million. Eleven years later you would have turned that investment into a puny £35 million. Not many career plans have a goal of losing £29 million a year for over a decade. Things change, so that means you need to learn not only how to make a plan but how to change that plan.

CASE STUDY

Ashwin and Alvey went into business together, opening an upmarket café restaurant. After a slow start and many long hours of hard work, the business began building. Things really took off, after an anonymous online review in 2007 raved about their food. Their plan had always been to build a brand, and a chain of restaurants. With several years of steadily increasing profitability, they had no problem in obtaining a series of bank loans, and quickly opened a further four restaurants. Then the credit crunch hit in 2008. Ashwin and Alvey's customers stopped eating out at the very time the banks called in their loans. In 2009, they declared bankruptcy. What they learned along the way was very valuable, and both men found work, Ashwin as a restaurant manager, and Alvey as a chef. While catering for a private corporate party, Alvey met a film financier, and one thing led to another, and he now runs an international film-set catering operation, travelling the world and serving famous actors and directors.

Making and remaking career plans

Once upon a time, we were told that to have a successful career we needed to write a career plan. A career plan set out what we were hoping to achieve and how we were going to get there. The more detailed plans might have even broken this down to a month-by-month set of actions. When should you be applying for a promotion, moving to a new company and so on?

Plans can be useful as they help us to think through the direction that we want to move in and what might be involved in moving. But the problem with plans is that by the time a few months have passed, so much has changed. Perhaps the industry that you were interested in has experienced a major collapse (who'd have thought that the banks would hit so much trouble in 2008) or perhaps you've changed: got married, had a child or just decided that this job isn't as much fun as you thought. In most cases, sticking rigidly to a career plan makes us less flexible and less able to make the most of opportunities. So, if career plans are not as useful we used to think, what is the alternative?

We need to develop what we call Planmanship skills. These are the skills to **R**evise, **A**bandon, **P**ause, **I**mplement, **D**evise, **C**opy, **P**romote and **R**evive a plan – our **RAPID-CPR** model. Nobody teaches you how to do this. Until now.

Applying RAPID-CPR

Revising a plan. Plans need constant monitoring to see if they are still working. Generally we only monitor plans for progress, and our only remedy is to work harder. However, revising a plan requires us to consider the:

- destination
- route
- method of transport.

Questions to regularly ask about your career plan

- Is the destination still attainable from where you are now?
- Is there a better destination that you have discovered along the way?
- Is the route ahead clear? If not, are the barriers surmountable?

- Is there a better, faster, more efficient route?
- Is there a more 'scenic' route that will be more pleasurable or provide a richer learning experience?
- Is the way I am trying to get there the most appropriate?
- Should I be doing this on my own or should I enlist partners, colleagues or supporters?
- Should I ditch some underperforming partners, colleagues or supporters?
- What else should I be doing, or doing better, to get to where I want to be?

Abandoning a plan. Sometimes giving up is not failure. That great American comedian W.C. Fields once said, 'If at first you don't succeed, try again, then give up, there is no point in being a damn fool about it.' To give up a plan can require courage; and failure can be reframed as endeavour rather than disgrace. We have to overcome that sense that quitters are losers. After all, nobody who quit gambling or smoking is a loser.

Questions to ask before you abandon a career plan or plough on regardless

- Do I still want the planned outcome?
- Have I tried revising the plan?
- Have I given the plan sufficient time to work?
- Have I got a better alternative?
- What are the risks of continuing with the plan?
- What are the risks of abandoning it?
- Are there others depending upon me to deliver this plan? If so, how can I minimise the impact on them, or provide them with a better alternative?
- Is the plan worth keeping for another time?

Pausing a plan. Sometimes it is just not the right time for your plan. Technology companies talk about the leading edge and the bleeding edge. The former is a great place to be; the latter, as the term implies, can be painful and unsuccessful. Launching a business as the credit crunch hits; proposing the purchase of an office cat when your boss is a cat hater; and listening to the music of Barry Manilow are all plans that need to be paused.

Questions to ask before you pause or continue with a career plan

- Do I have the support in terms of budget, management buy-in or other forms of backing necessary for the plan to succeed?
- How much of my political capital/my colleagues' patience will I exhaust in pursuing the plan?
- Are there clear circumstances evident that pose a threat to my plan that are likely to recede in the foreseeable future?
- Is any disruption caused by pausing the plan outweighed by the benefits of pausing the plan?
- If I pause the plan, will I have access to the same support in future to relaunch it?

Implementing a plan. The thinking is easy, the doing is a lot harder. As Pablo Picasso once said, 'What one does is what counts. Not what one had the intention of doing.'

Dr Johnson said, 'Nothing will be achieved, if first all objections must be overcome' and with his casual chic, Richard Branson said more or less the same thing: 'Screw it, let's do it.' In other words, the biggest threat to the success of a plan, is you failing to implement it.

Questions to ask when implementing a career plan

- What am I scared of?
- What obstacles could I realistically face?
- What possible obstacles might I face?

- How can I prepare to overcome any obstacles?
- Am I scared of the plan failing?
- What do I feel about failure?
- How could I feel more positive about failure should it happen?
- Am I scared of the plan succeeding?
- What sources of support can I muster to increase the chances of success?
- What or who is likely to derail the plan, and how can I address these threats?
- How can I align my plan with the best interests of colleagues or existing popular initiatives?
- How can I get senior buy-in to support and protect the plan?
- What small steps can I take to initiate the plan now?
- What small experiments or pilots could I undertake to get things going?

Devising a plan. Two of the biggest problems that people experience with their career are that you feel stuck or that you are drifting. Creating a plan can help you to get unstuck and stop drifting. Plans may not predict the future but they can get you started and give you purpose and direction.

The trouble with plans is that you may not be sure what the solution to your problem is. Sometimes we are even unsure what problem we are trying to solve. Other times we feel as though our plans have to solve all of our problems, or they are not worth bothering with. We need to recognise that plans that have outcomes more than a few months into the future are likely to have unpredictable and unanticipated outcomes. This is not a reason not to get going on a plan, but a reminder that we need to be flexible in how we plan and expect the unexpected. To devise a plan, we need to agree on a destination, a route and a method of transport. In other words, we need to agree on the where, the which way and the how of achieving our plans.

CASE STUDY

Vik was lost in his career until by chance he stumbled across a YouTube video about chicken sexing. He had a strange feeling that he should try his hand at this noble art. Vik knew where he wanted to go, but had no idea of the pathway to his dream, or the method of getting there. After seeing a career counsellor, he confirmed his goal, and discovered that many sexers come from, or are trained in, Japan – where the techniques were perfected. However, this was impractical for Vik, and he managed to find a company closer to home that would train him. He also discovered that his training would be hands-on. So Vik had a destination, a route to his desired job and a method of travelling the pathway to the job. He had a plan.

Questions to ask when devising a career plan

- What do I want to do?
- What can I do?
- What can I do with the help of others?
- What first steps could I take?
- How would things be different if everything turns out the way I expect?
- Where do I want to get to?
- What other destinations might be acceptable alternatives if things change?
- Am I prepared to end up in a totally different and as yet unknown destination?
- What is the best route that I can see at this time, to get going?
- Will I take the well-worn path or the path less travelled?
- If there is a fork in the road, what will I do? If it is a case of the lesser of two evils, do I do the one I haven't done before?
- How I am going to get started?
- Who else should I involve?
- (How) can I delegate tasks?
- Is time an important factor?

- How can I manage my expectations about time and the fact that delays might be inevitable?
- Can I break down my plan into a series of discrete plans, that can ensure some progress even if subsequent plans fail?

Copying a plan. Imitation is the sincerest form of flattery. When making a plan, it is a great idea to see what is already working for others. It will save you time in reinventing the wheel. Copying has a bad name, because we are told it is dishonest. On the other hand the world would not function without it. An apprentice plumber and a trainee surgeon are supposed to copy and reproduce the techniques they are being taught. Most different models of car from every manufacturer tend to have a wheel in each corner, and a wheel in front of the driver's seat. Most social media sites now have a 'like' button. The poet T.S. Eliot said, 'Immature poets imitate; mature poets steal; bad poets deface what they take, and good poets make it into something better, or at least something different.' Often Eliot's quote is shortened to imply that stealing is all you need to do. However, the longer quote reveals that really effective plans are ones that build on the ideas and plans of others, and are adapted for your own needs; they are not carbon copies. Before you plan or revise a plan, do your homework and see what others are doing in the same space first.

Questions to ask when copying a career plan

- Who are the most successful people in my desired area?
- What are they doing?
- What are the key features of their plans and strategies?
- How could I adapt their plans to my circumstances?
- What could I add or take away to make another's plan more viable for me?
- How could I find out about the plans that people I admire employ?
- Who could share their plans and wisdom to enhance my own plans and wisdom?
- Are there some tried and trusted ways of doing what I want to do?

- How could I experiment with the traditional or accepted ways of doing things to do something more creative and original?
- How could I combine elements of other people's plans with my own thoughts to produce something greater?

Promoting a plan. Sometimes we can be talked out of our plans too easily. We have all regretted a time when we gave up too quickly on what we wanted to do. Are you the person who:

- chose the wrong career because they thought it would please their parents
- stayed in a role they despised because their partner wasn't willing to take a risk
- tried for a qualification or occupation that they weren't really interested in out of a fear of social embarrassment
- did not apply for a role because they accepted poor advice confidently delivered.

Sometimes we have to argue for our plans, promote them to other people to persuade them to support us or, at the very least, get out of our way. To do this, we need to be able to know what our plans are in detail; to anticipate objections and address them; and to know the weak spots, and either acknowledge them or explain how these parts of the plan will be managed.

Questions to ask to promote your career plan

- What is my plan in a nutshell?
- What am I trying to achieve?
- Why is this such a good idea?
- What benefits flow from achieving my goals?
- How do they benefit others?
- Are there better plans and, if so, why have I chosen this plan?
- How can I manage any weak spots in my plan?
- What support or commitment is required from other people?
- How can I make it easy for others to support or commit to the plan?
- Do I need to own the plan, or is it strategic to let another take the credit for the plan?

Reviving a plan. Sometimes, it is necessary or sensible to dust off an older plan and try again. The success of a plan very often comes down to timing. Edison did not invent the lightbulb: there were about 20 inventors prior to Edison. But Edison was in the right place at the right time for the invention to take off. Similar stories can be told about many other popular inventions, including the telephone (it was not Alexander Graham Bell, rather Antonio Meucci), the iPod (Kane Kramer invented a portable digital music player 20 years before Apple) – and on it goes. So there is no shame in going back to a plan. Maybe it worked well then, and its time has come around again (like vinyl records and typewriters – both experiencing a resurgence). Perhaps the plan failed before, but now the time is right. All of this suggests, at the very least, to keep a record of your plans – both successful and unsuccessful – because you never know when it might come in handy!

Questions to ask yourself about reviving your old career plans

■ What have I tried in the past that might work in these circumstances?
■ What has changed that might permit my plan to work this time around?
■ How could I justify reviving a plan that has failed in the past?
■ What did I learn the last time around using this plan that I could usefully apply now?

Planfulness requires regular RAPID-CPR

Our RAPID-CPR model should be thought of as a way of continually managing career plans. In the world of social media, where things change continuously, there are always going to be opportunities to try new or old plans. There will always be the need to revise plans, promote plans and sometimes abandon them.

Being positive about change

Everyone seems to bang on about embracing change and how change is great, to the point that it can grate. There are lots of examples where change is not necessarily a good thing. New Coke was not better than old Coke, and social media sites have regularly had to reverse so-called 'improvements' in the face of widespread user anger. For instance, in 2013 Twitter changed the way that blocking abusive users worked, before changing their minds only hours later after a torrent of negative feedback.

However, as the quote at the beginning of this chapter implied, change is inevitable. It is the natural way of things. As Cardinal John Newman pointed out, 'To live is to change.' We are continually changing. Our cells regenerate, we age, and, over time, we can tire of some things and be excited by others. While not all change is positive, a lot of it is – advances in medical science give babies and their mothers far more chance of living than they did only a century ago.

Our attitudes to change are paradoxical. We find change difficult, yet most of us like surprises.

Why is change so difficult?

Why do we find change so difficult? The answer to that could fill several books, and it probably has. One major reason is that change requires effort. Human beings, indeed all living beings, have the capacity to learn. Learning something means that on each occasion you practise, you do whatever you've learned faster or with less mental or physical effort. Eventually, there are many things we end up doing without having to think about it. We develop a routine that does not require much effort on our part to follow. If we know that Sundays means roast beef for lunch, pretty quickly we find we can cook it and the Yorkshire puddings without consulting Delia Smith at every step. Eventually, we even stop burning it. We are creatures of habit.

However, our routines can be thrown into disarray if the butcher runs out of beef or if we invite vegetarians to lunch! Now we have to pull out a vegetarian recipe book, and familiarise ourselves with things such as nutloaf. In other words, we have to put some effort in, and because we are making a new recipe for the first time, we worry whether it will come out right. The positive that comes out of this experience is that we have learned some new recipes and cooking techniques, and we have something of value to offer carnivores and vegetarians alike.

It is the same with work. Embracing change results in learning new skills and developing increased knowledge. This in turn increases our marketability to employers. We have more to offer. And it gets even better. The more often we embrace change and engage in learning, the better we become at the process of learning. Through school, the exams might have become progressively more high-pressured, but we got better at revising the more exams we took. There is plenty of research to suggest that the more exams you take, the better at exams you become.

The alternative is to do nothing or resist. Sometimes, this can be the best strategy; but resisting change will often result in you being left behind or alienating colleagues and your employer. This is especially true if you are a lone voice who is hanging on to the past. We have all met the person who insists on doing it 'their way' and refuses to embrace new ways of doing things. All too often that person is the one who is 'managed out' of the business, sidelined or, sometimes, sacked.

Embracing change means embracing failure

Another reason we find change so challenging is fear of failure. If change requires learning, and learning involves trial and error, then change can become a trial for some people who fear making errors. Try thinking about errors in the way that industrialist John Paul Getty saw them. He famously said, 'If you are not failing, you are not trying hard enough.' In other words, the way to progress is to keep trying things, knowing that you will win some and lose some. In fact, it is generally the case that we learn far more from failures than we do from successes. Failures teach us the limits of our capacity or knowledge, or about the way things are organised that we had not appreciated.

People who fear failure are far more likely to stick to familiar routines and never try anything new. Taken to extremes, this kind of behaviour can become debilitating. For instance, there was a teacher of our acquaintance who had a particular and unchanging suit-and-tie combination for each day of the week. All went well until the local dry cleaners contrived to lose 'Thursday's' tie. He could not settle until he had tracked down the very same tie to maintain his routine!

Alternatively, risk avoiders can fall into the trap of putting off trying to do something until the necessity to act becomes overwhelming. They then make an impulsive and irrational decision that rarely ends well, and reinforces their conviction to avoid novelty in the future. Whether it is waiting for ages for Mr Right and ending up with Mr I Don't Know What She Was Thinking, or a cat pussyfooting about before making a fatal leap that pulls the curtains off the wall, the no-change-to-extreme-change approach is best avoided.

Embracing change also means accepting that failure is an inevitable part of life that can help us more quickly solve problems. Think about failure as a bit like exploring a maze. If you don't risk failure by exploring a path in the maze, you would never get anywhere. As with learning, the more small failures you experience, the better practised you become at retrieving yourself from the situation – and the better you become at contingency planning to get back on track.

The benefits of embracing change

Lifelong learning perspective	Committing to acquiring new skills and knowledge continuously will increase your chances of remaining in or finding work.
Greater adaptability	The more frequently you embrace change and the more you practise the skills of adapting to change, the more adaptable you will be.
Greater market currency and value	Acquiring and maintaining an ever increasing skill-set will make you more valuable to employers.
Enhanced competitiveness	Employers operate in a fast-changing environment, so they like employing staff who are able to thrive on change.
Increased chances of employment	The more adaptable you are, the more opportunities there will be for you in different roles.
Intellectual stimulation	Continuously learning new information and skills is stimulating!
Increased work efficiency	Having a big set of up-to-date skills will allow you to be more efficient at work.
Stronger and more effective networks	Change is generally something that happens to groups as well as individuals. Being positive about change may assist your colleagues to come to terms with change and can enhance your networks and bonds at work.

More efficient learner	The best way to learn is to practise learning regularly.
Greater resilience and bounce-back strategies	Embracing change will involve failing from time to time. The more often you fail, the better you will become at bouncing back.

Social media and change

Nowhere is the need to embrace change stronger than in interacting with social media. No sooner have we learned to laugh out loud ('lol') at the witty postings of our colleagues than we learn from a Facebook report in 2015 that we are hopelessly out of date. 'Lol' appears less than 2% of the time in posts, whereas 'haha' is the preferred expression in over 50% of posts. While this may seem a particularly trivial example, when presenting a professional image in social media, we do not want to be the virtual equivalent of the person in the office in the safari suit and pipe.

Social media has changed dramatically over the last decade. The graphic on page 22 highlights some of the major changes. (It should be noted that LinkedIn followed a similar path after being established in 2003, and by 2014 had over 330 million members.)

You can see from the illustration just how many different platforms now exist, including MySpace, Facebook, LinkedIn, Twitter, YouTube, Google Plus, Tumblr, Instagram, Pinterest, Snapchat, Foursquare and WhatsApp. If you are likely to work in other markets, such as Russia and China, be aware of their alternatives, such as vk.com, which is often called the Russian Facebook; Renren (China); or of media focused on particular groups, such as MyMFB, a 'Facebook alternative' for Muslims.

Some platforms change and thrive, while others become more narrowly focused. The site Secret came, dazzled and crashed within 18 months, and MySpace lost many people to Facebook but has a particularly strong following with musicians.

 YEARS

EVOLUTION OF SOCIAL
2004 - 2014

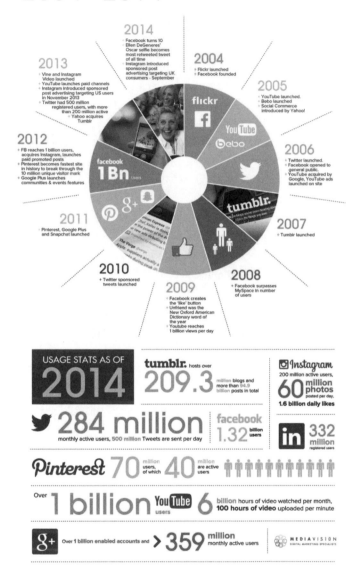

2014
- Facebook turns 10
- Ellen DeGeneres' Oscar selfie becomes most retweeted tweet of all time
- Instagram introduced sponsored post advertising targeting UK consumers - September

2004
- Flickr launched
- Facebook founded

2005
- YouTube launched
- Bebo launched
- Social Commerce introduced by Yahoo!

2013
- Vine and Instagram Video launched
- YouTube launches paid channels
- Instagram introduced sponsored post advertising targeting US users in November 2013
- Twitter had 500 million registered users, with more than 200 million active
- Yahoo acquires Tumblr

2006
- Twitter launched
- Facebook opened to general public
- YouTube acquired by Google, YouTube ads launched on site

2012
- FB reaches 1 billion users, acquires Instagram, launches paid promoted posts
- Pinterest becomes fastest site in history to break through the 10 million unique visitor mark
- Google Plus launches communities & events features

2011
- Pinterest, Google Plus and Snapchat launched

2007
- Tumblr launched

2010
- Twitter sponsored tweets launched

2009
- Facebook creates the 'like' button
- Unfriend was the New Oxford American Dictionary word of the year
- Youtube reaches 1 billion views per day

2008
- Facebook surpasses MySpace in number of users

USAGE STATS AS OF 2014

tumblr. hosts over **209.3** million blogs and more than 94.9 billion posts in total

Instagram 200 million active users, **60 million** photos posted per day, **1.6 billion daily likes**

🐦 **284 million** monthly active users, 500 million Tweets are sent per day

facebook 1.32 billion users

in 332 million registered users

Pinterest 70 million users, of which **40** million are active users

Over **1 billion** YouTube users **6** billion hours of video watched per month, **100 hours of video** uploaded per minute

g+ Over 1 billion enabled accounts and **> 359** million monthly active users

MEDIAVISION DIGITAL MARKETING SPECIALISTS

© MediaVision. Used with permission.

Learning to adapt

Adaptability is the key to successful engagement in social media. This means:

- keeping up to date with new features and policies on existing sites
- keeping abreast of new entrants into the field of social media
- tailoring your content for different social media platforms (e.g. Facebook, LinkedIn and Twitter).

With existing sites, you need to keep an eye out for changes in policies and features. While the idea of reading a privacy policy may fill you with the same amount of dread as visiting a dentist with a penchant for sadism and a particularly squeaky drill, this task will pay dividends if it prevents you from displaying your personal opinions or photos to all and sundry (sundry often includes your employer and potential future employers!).

We suggest that you approach social media as you might the local village gossip, assuming that anything you say will spread through the village at the speed of light. In the case of social media, the village is of the global variety. This makes privacy concerns a priority. Do not expect social media companies to act in your best interest. Collecting, sharing and selling your information is a big part of their business model. They will encourage you to share, and sometimes they change their privacy policies in ways that can leave you vulnerable to people seeing information you thought had hitherto been protected. Your personal data can also 'leak' to advertisers or others when using apps in Facebook, completing tests or quizzes or even 'liking' a link or page. If you are tagged in photos, others whom you have specifically blocked or limited may gain access via a friend. Regularly reading privacy policies and checking your settings is an essential way of adapting to successful social media use.

New entrants appear on the scene regularly and it is worth taking an interest in who is who in the zoo. Unless your job directly depends on having up-to-date knowledge of all social media, it is unlikely that new social media sites will require your attention immediately. It is best to play a waiting game and see how the site is embraced by others. You might lose bragging rights about being one of the founding fathers, but you will also save valuable time by avoiding setting up profiles on obscure sites that are destined to fail. In fact, making a big thing of being on a left-field site that closes down quickly could give others the impression that you lack judgement. A great tip here is to be sure to have in your network a colleague who loves to be up to date with the very latest trends. This allows you to keep abreast of developments without having to commit to using every new site or service.

One of the best indicators that it is time to join a site is when you start to receive more than several invitations to join from your colleagues. This is a good sign that your audience – people in similar work to you – use the site. Second, sites that are mentioned regularly in the mainstream media indicate good starting points. All things being equal, the obvious ones are Facebook, LinkedIn and Twitter.

Once you have an account, you need to be on the lookout for new features. These come around from time to time and can provide fantastic opportunities to enhance your social media presence. For instance, LinkedIn introduced a feature called Pulse in 2013. This new feature provides a feed of articles that are of relevance to your profile, and also, importantly, the opportunity to write articles yourself that may promote your expertise and profile. This is a significant development for LinkedIn and a great opportunity for budding writers.

Should I invest my time in online tools that may not even be around in five years' time? Yes, because ...

- established sites such as Facebook and LinkedIn have proven they have lasted the distance, and have been going for over a decade so far
- five years is a long time in the world of work, and you can achieve a lot of things to benefit your career in that time
- not turning up to the party will mark you down as out of touch
- the skills and techniques you learn using a platform will set you up to get the most out of the next big thing
- you will make valuable contacts that enhance your network and your career
- your contacts from the old platform are more likely to migrate with you to the new platform, giving you a flying start.

Learning to use new software and tools

There is a language to social media that needs to be learned. It is the world of 'likes', 'friends', 'contacts', 'messages', 'updates', 'tweets', 'retweets', 'shares', and many many more. We have included an internet-to-English dictionary at the back of the book that you may find helpful to consult.

One way of approaching new software and tools is to understand the underlying metaphor driving the site. So with Twitter, the name and logo make it clear we are entering a world of birdsong. As with birdsong, our messages come in small bursts (tweets), and sometimes they are relayed (retweeted). Facebook is a relaxed community of 'friends', whereas LinkedIn is more the formal office environment where we have 'connections'. In Pinterest, we are in the arts and crafts world, or at least a noticeboard world, where we pin items of interest – here, the visual aspect of the information is of primary concern.

Understanding what these sites are trying to achieve can be a big help in understanding how to use them. The first thing you might do with any site could be to 'lurk' – which means to look in on what is going on without signing up. This can be a valuable way of understanding how the site works in outline, and that may help you decide on appropriate user names and your first contributions if and when you sign up. Some sites will allow this, such as Twitter, which allows you to search and read tweets without signing up, whereas others, including Facebook, require you to create an account to do anything.

Creating an account with social media sites can vary from quick and painless to painfully drawn out. Remember, a lot of social media sites (if not all) want as much of your personal data as possible, because they can market this to advertisers. In addition, some sites, such as LinkedIn, are based upon your 'online CV', so completing your profile for this site can take as long as it does to write a CV. A good tip is to have an electronic version of your CV open when you sign up, so that you can cut and paste job titles, years, educational institutions, qualifications, awards, publications, etc into the profile.

Nearly all social media sites give you the option of including a photograph. So, before completing your profile, ensure you have a professional looking photograph ready to upload.

The popular social media sites have improved beyond recognition in recent years in their usability. This means that you do not need to worry about your computer skills too much in order to get going on the sites.

How do I keep up with all the new social media gimmicks?

■ Google and read articles on social media trends.
■ Unless your career goal is to be a social media guru, aim to be where the rest of your herd is, because they don't get the latest gimmicks yet either.
■ Don't put all your eggs in one social media basket – spread the love across at least three platforms.
■ Experiment with features to understand how they work and how effective they are.
■ Don't be afraid to ask questions on social media about new features.
■ Ignore features or gimmicks that add nothing to your media presence.
■ Make friends with someone who follows the latest trends like a hawk.

Doesn't building a social media profile take a lot of time and effort (which I can't afford)? Is it really worth it?

The fact that you are reading this book suggests that you already have an interest in social media. The short answer is that it does not take such a large amount of time or effort to get a basic social media profile set up – and the rewards can be great. Indeed, the authors of this book first met through social media before becoming friends and colleagues in real life. Simply put, if getting a new job, promotion, contract, customer, reader, listener or business is of no value to you; or if learning new things about the world around you, or being rapidly informed of world events as they happen holds no interest for you, either you are devoid of all vital signs, or social media may not be for you. For the rest of us – and that is just about everybody – social media of one form or another is not only recommended, it is practically essential.

How do you find the time?

Social media first came onto the scene for most of us in the early 2000s with MySpace, Facebook and LinkedIn, but it has been about in less user-friendly guises since the 1970s. To start with, most people ignored it, or thought it was something for nerds or teenagers. Fast forward to the present and even the Queen and the Pope are tweeting and agreeing to be in selfies! If these good folks in their 70s and 80s can get to grips with social media and make the time, so can you!

Ok, so you don't have an entourage or marketing department to send out tweets of your latest concert dates or publicity stunt, but that doesn't give you the excuse to ignore the medium. Think of social media like a meal: we all need to eat, but when we are short of time we might just grab a sandwich. In the same way, engaging with social media can occupy most of your day or just be something that you dip into for five minutes.

As with any other routine activity, you need to manage the amount of time that you spend on social media. Think through your daily or weekly routine and work out what time could be devoted to social media. Given that we can access social media from pretty much anywhere on phones and tablets, there may be plenty of opportunities to engage with social media that aren't suitable for other business or personal activities.

A survey published in 2013 found that, an average, folk in the UK spent less time engaging with social media than most of the other 24 countries sampled (1.5 hours per day compared to an international average of 2.5 hours per day).[iii]

Unsurprisingly, the under-35s used social media for twice as long as the 50–64-year olds (3.3 hours per day compared to 1.6 hours per day). Nonetheless, the statistics show just how important social media has become in the lives of most people. The time indicated is longer than estimates from the United

States Department of Agriculture of the average time an American spends in 'formal' eating each day (67 minutes).[iv]

How long does it take?

Each activity doesn't take long. Try it out!

Read a tweet	5 seconds
Send a tweet	20 seconds
Send a photo tweet	25 seconds
Read a Facebook post	20 seconds
Post a Facebook update	60 seconds–2 minutes
Read a LinkedIn post	20 seconds–2 minutes
Post a LinkedIn update	2 minutes–4 minutes
Post a LinkedIn Pulse article (a brand new article including writing it)	30 minutes–2 hours
Respond to a blog post	2 minutes
Write a blog post	10 minutes–2 hours

When you think about it, social media does not need to take up a lot of your time. You can post contributions as quickly as it takes to press the photograph button on your smartphone, or as long as it takes to compose 140 characters of text. Indeed, that is one of the features that have caused so many to get in trouble posting ill-considered and impulsive content! Thankfully, most of us would never consider being so impulsive as to walk around Sainsbury's in our speedos, let alone taking and posting a selfie of ourselves in the frozen veg section. So, apply the same restraint to social media in order to avoid people thinking you are crazy or a terrible show-off.

In thinking about your day, you might decide to read and send tweets between meetings (or even in them if it is done surreptitiously!). However, writing articles to post online may take a lot longer and is something that you may wish to schedule more formally by setting aside a couple of hours at the same time each week, so you can blog regularly.

Like anything in life, if you do not prioritise social media, you will end up not doing it.

How long do I have to keep doing this until I get to see some real results?

We have all read the hype about social media – that all we need to do is film Tiddles scowling, pop it up on YouTube, and you and your cat will be more famous than Miley Bieber-Kardashian. Unless you already have the following and notoriety of a celebrity, it is probably best to revise your expectations. Social media has replaced making hit records as many people's fantasy route to overnight stardom – you might get lucky, but then again you might win the lottery. Chris Wilson, writing on the website Slate.com, found that of 10,000 YouTube videos uploaded, only 0.3% had more than 10,000 views, whereas 65% had less than 50 views. Only one got over the 100,000 mark.[v] While 100,000 views is fantastic, you only have a one in 10,000 chance of achieving that, and the odds drop off exponentially as you start thinking about the millions or tens of millions posted. The lottery may be a viable alternative.

That said, most people don't need anything like that level of engagement to enjoy a boost in their career prospects from social media. A well-targeted post attracting 30 views and five likes might be sufficient to bring you to the attention of a key decision-maker in your field.

There is one now well-established strategy for increasing social media attention, and that is to engage regularly with social media. Engagement means:

- writing regular posts
- sharing updates
- frequently tweeting
- sharing and appreciating the content of others with likes, retweets and shares
- developing conversations with your followers
- demonstrating that there is a human being behind the social media façade.

Regular short, targeted posts are essential. Do not start blogging if you are going to give up after a few short weeks or months. All you are likely to do is irritate and disappoint those that have started to follow you. Do not worry if you do not have a lot of followers to start with.

The best way to build a presence on social media

- Be persistent. Post regularly. Post about things relevant to your industry. Your choice of breakfast or your cat's doings are unlikely to be relevant.
- Be positive. 'Like' other people's work, and make positive comments.
- Be a follower. Follow others and they are likely to follow you back. However, do ensure that those you choose to follow are appropriate for the professionalism you wish to convey.
- Join discussion groups and join in. Ensure your comments are well informed, positive and appropriately supportive.

Remember, even if your early posts receive an underwhelming response, the beauty of social media is that people can come back to your posts, weeks, months or years later. Like discovering the back catalogue of a favourite artist, your once overlooked posts may spring to life much later and when you least expect it.

IN A NUTSHELL

The world of work is changing rapidly and this is reflected most strongly in how social media has already become central to many people's work and increasingly is the backdrop to our lives. Social media offers an exciting new world to explore and to exploit to further your career. To get the most out of social media, and to develop your career successfully, understanding that the world is changing and how to best embrace that change is critical.

Getting involved in social media, becoming a presence on social sites, and learning the language of social media are all increasingly important to build the networks that will serve your career and to be noticed by recruiters.

Getting to grips with the new rules of work and social media, by becoming an adventurous explorer of this exciting and rich virtual world, has the potential to turbo charge your career in real life too! Dive in!

2 INFORMATION IS POWER – COLLECT AS MUCH AS YOU CAN

This chapter will encourage you to think about what information exists online that can support your career building. It will show you how to find out about different careers, find opportunities and jobs and keep up to date. It will introduce you to searches, alerts and networks as three ways in which you can find the information that you need and will argue that you need all three to be effective. It will also encourage you to think about how you manage and keep track of information.

This chapter will cover:

■ researching jobs and career options

■ how to ask the right questions in order to find job opportunities

■ how to search smartly

■ how to find the answer to questions you haven't yet asked using alerts and networks

■ dealing with information overload.

Why do you need information for your career?

An early name for the internet was 'the information superhighway'. The internet pioneers dreamed of a world where large quantities of information could be easily transferred around the globe and where it would also be freely available at a low (or no) cost to all. This dream has largely been realised with profound consequences for society and for our careers.

In the context of our careers we use information for a range of purposes.

■ To explore and make decisions about jobs and careers we are interested in.
■ To find opportunities, such as jobs, volunteering and further study, that we might actively pursue.
■ To enhance our knowledge and expertise in order to increase our chances of success when we apply for jobs.

If you are well informed you will have a good basis for making career decisions, be able to spot opportunities quicker and appear more knowledgeable when you go for a job. The process of researching and using information is also a key employability skill in and of itself which is applicable to most jobs.

Collecting career-related information is a good strategy to help you enhance your career. If you are skilled at collecting information you will find opportunities more regularly than everyone else. The internet has made this process of collecting easier than ever before. In the past, researching career information required you to buy newspapers, visit libraries, research employer requirements and perhaps even learn to access complex statistics; now, the internet puts a vast amount of information at your fingertips.

In the past the main problem with research was finding any information. Internet search engines have made this problem vanish and replaced it with an equally difficult one: how can you find anything useful among the huge amount of information that you can easily access? This chapter will discuss how to find information, how to avoid getting overwhelmed by it and how to put it to work when you are building your career.

CASE STUDY

Joe feels that his job searching is going nowhere. He resolves to engage with the internet more. He starts by searching in Google but gradually works out that the best opportunities in his field are on www.jobs4logistics.com, which lists opportunities from the logistics field. He also subscribes to key news sources in the field, such as warehousenews.co.uk, so that he can keep up to date with the industry.

To save himself time he accesses the site's alert feature and starts to receive emails every Monday morning telling him what new jobs have been listed. He also tells a few of his contacts that he is interested in finding out more about how other companies organise their recruitment to see how it relates to his own company. This results in people sending him more information about where jobs in his field are listed online.

Joe is starting to build up a lot of information about the jobs that are available in his field. He finds himself getting distracted at work by this and resolves to review all of these opportunities each Thursday night. He starts to feel much more confident that there is a job out there for him somewhere.

Search: How can I find what I'm looking for?

When you think about searching for information on the internet one word looms large: GOOGLE.

Google is an important way of finding information for your career, but it isn't the only way or necessarily the most useful. We will initially look at making the most of Google before going on to look at more specific career sites.

Why can't I find any jobs relevant to me by Googling?
Google is an amazing tool. It makes finding complex information simple. However, as with any tool you can use it well or badly.

A few years ago researchers at the University of Derby ran an experiment with groups of students and unemployed workers.[vi] They asked them to use the internet to find out about the career opportunities that were available to them. Almost all of them went straight to Google. What was interesting was that they asked Google questions as if it was a person.

Google isn't a person – it is a very sophisticated set of computers which will try to interpret questions like the one above and provide you with an answer. But, if you want to get the most out of Google you need to know how to talk Googleese.

Basic Googleese

Google produces better quality results when you use keywords rather than asking an actual question. So, start by thinking about what the keywords in your question are, and just type those into Google.

When you are thinking of keywords you need to consider how other people might describe what you are looking for. For example, if you want to search for information about getting paid more, try a search for *improving pay* but also use words that businesses might use, such as *reward* and *remuneration*.

Using keywords can be tricky. The problem is that not everyone thinks exactly the same way that you do, which means that your keywords might not help you to access jobs and resources that have been described with different words (even if they mean something similar). Thankfully, there are a couple of techniques that you can adopt to help you overcome this problem.

- **Thesaurusing.** Put the search terms you are thinking of using into an online thesaurus to see if there are other words you could use.
- **Multi-passing.** If your first keywords don't work then find the link that seems to be the nearest to what you are looking for and browse the site for other search terms you could use. Now make a second pass with those search terms and pick the best fit site to do the same again.

An alternative problem is finding that the words that you are using are too common and they give you too many results on Google. One response to this is to use double quotation marks to join words together so that Google focuses on the things that you are interested in.

So "electronic engineering" will only provide results that focus on electronic engineering, rather than results that focus on electronics and/or engineering.

Tricks for getting the most out of Google

- Use *site:* to search a particular website, e.g. *engineer vacancies site: www.rolls-royce.com* will search the Rolls-Royce site for any engineering vacancies.
- Use * to replace any words or letters that you don't know, e.g. *all work and no play makes * a dull boy'.* You can also use this to search for words that have different spellings; so *wom*n network* will find mentions of networks that include both the word *woman* and *women.*
- Use the minus sign, '–', to remove words that you don't want included in the search, e.g. when you search for the word *promotion* you will often find that you get a lot of results related to marketing promotions. Using the phrase *promotion – marketing* eliminates these.
- Do other kinds of search. Once you've searched for something, Google brings up a range of options for more specialised kinds of search. These can allow you to search just for news sites, for things to buy (shopping), for images and so on.

Google and the Google logo are registered trademarks of Google Inc., used with permission.

■ Make use of Google's Advanced Search feature. This allows you to specify your searches with a lot more precision.

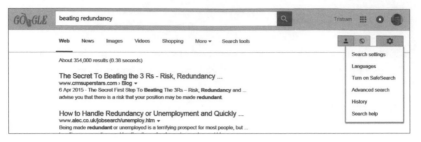

Google and the Google logo are registered trademarks of Google Inc., used with permission.

Google and the Google logo are registered trademarks of Google Inc., used with permission.

What other search engines should I use beyond Google?

Despite the power of Google, it is important to recognise that it is not the only search engine out there. There are a range of other search engines that you can use, many of which are more specialised than Google.

Five search engines beyond Google

1. **Bananaslug** (www.bananaslug.com) throws a wildcard term into your searches, which means that you can find things that would never crop

---

up in a standard Google search.

2. **Boardreader** (www.boardreader.com) searches forums and discussion boards.
3. **Duck Duck Go** (www.duckduckgo.com) is an alternative to Google that promises a greater level of privacy. Unlike Google, it does not track your online behaviour or attempt to personalise your searches.
4. **Meltwater icerocket** (www.icerocket.com) searches blogs.
5. **Social searcher** (www.social-searcher.com) searches social media.

So Google is a pretty good tool for general searches, but you might want to look beyond it for more specific kinds of searches.

The tools that are available are changing all the time, so it is worth keeping your eyes open for new types of search engine. For example, there are now technologies that allow for the searching of images, audio and video. Some of these have already been turned into search engines for public use. We can expect this kind of search technology to become increasingly sophisticated over the next few years.

None of the tools that we have discussed so far are career specific. However, there are a number of career-specific search engines that you might consider using, such as **ZipRecruiter** (www.ziprecruiter.com) or **Indeed** (www.indeed.co.uk). These search engines typically search multiple jobs boards and company websites to find opportunities. However, at present many of the job-focused search engines have limited geographical reach, and you may find that you are offered a lot of opportunities in America.

Job search engines are useful, but at present they are probably not sufficient for all of your career information needs. Thankfully, there are websites that are specifically set up to allow people to search for career information. It is possible to group these into a number of main types (see table on page 40).

The type of site you choose to use will vary depending on what you are looking for. In general, the more developed your ideas about your career are, the more you will want to use a specific site.

Type of career website	What it does?	Example
General job boards	Sites on which employers post actual vacancies. These sites are gradually replacing newspapers as the main place that people find job vacancies. Some may include the opportunity to apply directly through the site.	**Monster** (www.monster.co.uk) is a huge international job and career site. In addition to listing vacancies for jobs in all sectors it also provides a large amount of career information and advice.
Industry-specific job boards	Sites that are focused on a particular industry or sector. These sites will only offer vacancies that relate to that sector. Some may include the opportunity to apply directly through the site.	**madjobs** (www.jobs.mad.co.uk) lists jobs specifically for the marketing, advertising and design industry.
Company-specific job boards	Job boards that relate to one organisation or an interrelated collection of organisations.	**NHS Careers** (www.nhscareers.nhs.uk) provides a huge amount of information about working in the National Health Service. This includes a live jobs board, which typically has thousands of jobs available.
Course information sites	Sites that provide information about courses, qualifications and learning opportunities. Some may include the opportunity to apply directly through the site.	**UCAS** (www.ucas.com) is a site that provides course information and opportunities to directly apply for courses. While the site is best known for its university applications process, it is increasingly branching out and covering college and postgraduate applications as well.
Career exploration sites	Sites that provide more general kinds of information supporting career exploration rather than finding a particular job.	**iCould** (www.icould.com) is a careers website based around video stories. It is a great resource for people choosing careers or making a career change, but doesn't offer actual vacancy information.

Type of career website	What it does?	Example
Career-related social media sites	There are a growing number of sites that help you to make and maintain professional contacts. These sites will be discussed in more detail in Chapter 4.	**LinkedIn** (www.linkedin.com) is an online professional networking tool. It includes elements of career exploration and a general jobs board alongside the networking features of the site.

So, if you are sure that you want to work as a plumber, you definitely want to use a jobs board that is focused on construction vacancies (or ideally just on plumbing vacancies). Identifying and making use of a specialised resource like this will save you a lot of time and give you much better results than trying to use Google for this purpose.

There are an ever-growing number of career-related websites available. You may find that you need to use Google to find the one that is most useful to you and your career interests. However, it is also worth asking friends, colleagues and professional contacts which sites they use. As we will see, networking can be a very powerful way to find information that is useful for your career.

Note: Many career websites have their own tools for searching. As with using Google, you can use these search tools well or badly. Often they will have their own version of Googleese and Advance Search features that can help you to refine your searches. It is worth investigating these when you first visit a new site.

Five common search errors

It is easy to make mistakes when you are searching. Here are some common ones to watch out for.

1. **Spelling errors.** Many search engines try and correct basic spelling errors, but it is still worth checking your spelling to be sure that you've got it right. Searching for *career* and *carer* will give you very different results.

---

2. **Using overly general search terms.** Search engines require you to be specific. If you search for words such as *job* or *career* on their own, don't be surprised if you don't get back anything very useful.

3. **Beware the double meaning.** Some words have two meanings. You know that you are looking for jobs as a *buyer* in the retail sector but don't be surprised if Google throws up hundreds of irrelevant results relating to buying various products.

4. **Using full sentences.** Focus on keywords for the best results.

5. **Giving up too easily.** Search engines will offer you hundreds or even thousands of results. Take the time to look at more than the top one. You may even want to venture onto page 2 or 3 of the search results to see what you find there.

Alerts: How can I make sure I don't miss anything?

'Search' is a useful tool when you have got some time put aside for job searching or career exploration. However, the right job may not just be sitting there waiting for you to find it. Clever searching is important, but sometimes you will just have to wait until the right opportunity presents itself.

The problem with waiting for the right job to come along is that it then becomes very easy to miss it. If your dream job is advertised during a week when you are really busy in your current job, you may find that you forget to search and miss the opportunity.

One way to deal with this is to set up an *alert*. Alerts bring the information to you, usually by delivering information to your email. While it is possible to ask to be alerted about everything that happens on a particular website, increasingly alerts will allow you to specify what you want to be alerted about.

Not all career websites offer the opportunity to set up an alert, but it is becoming more common. Each site will have a different way of setting up an alert, but once you've mastered one you should find it increasingly easy to set up alerts from any sites that you use.

Fish4Jobs (www.fish4.co.uk) is an example of a site that offers an alert feature. The site refers to it as *'jobs by email'* on its main menu. When you choose this option you are invited to *'create a jobs by email alert'*. You are then presented with a form to fill in which looks very like the Advanced Search forms offered by many other search engines.

The Fish4Jobs email alert form asks you to insert some details about yourself and your email address. It then asks you a number of questions about the kinds of jobs you want to be alerted about.

- **Location.** You will need to add where you live and then specify how many miles you are willing to travel to work.
- **Sector.** You need to choose which employment sectors you are interested in working in.
- **Salary band.** You need to choose the salary that you will be willing to accept. Start with your minimum and tick all that apply up to the maximum that you think you are likely to get (and maybe just add one more for luck).
- **Contract type.** Do you want a permanent contract, a fixed-term contract or a temporary position? Again, tick all that you are willing to accept.
- **Hours.** Do you want to work full- or part-time (or either)?
- **Recruiter type.** Do you only want to see vacancies listed by employers or are you happy to also see vacancies listed by recruitment agencies?

Once you have specified the criteria for your jobs alert, you will then be sent a confirmation email; once you have confirmed and set up a password you will begin to be emailed jobs directly. Alerts work by emailing you any jobs that fit the criteria that you have specified. This can be tricky at first and you may find that you are receiving too many jobs (in which case you should log back in and narrow your criteria) or too few jobs (so you might need to be a bit more flexible, perhaps by lowering your salary expectations or increasing the distance you are willing to travel).

Most alerts on job boards work in a similar way to the Fish4Jobs one. However, there are two other main ways in which alerts can be organised.

Image made freely available for reproduction by the Mozilla Foundation.

1. **Really Simple Syndication (RSS)** is a technology that allows you to subscribe to a range of news feeds and to read them through an RSS reader (available from most app stores). RSS is declining in popularity, but it can offer you a neat way to bring all of your career-related information together.

   The key thing to look for with RSS is this symbol above. If you see that symbol you can click on it and then copy the URL in your web browser and paste it into your RSS Reader. An RSS Reader is a web service or piece of software that allows you to bring together a range of different RSS feeds so that you can read them in one place. In essence, it allows you to compile your own bespoke newspaper out of a range of things that interest you. There are lots of different RSS Readers available and they tend to change fairly often. Wikipedia has a really useful page (www.wikipedia.org/wiki/Comparison_of_feed_aggregators) which compares all of the currently available RSS Readers.

2. **Use of social media.** Increasingly, websites are offering linked social media accounts. So, for example, the job board Go2Jobs offers linked Facebook and Twitter accounts that relate to specific areas (e.g. Crawley Jobs on Facebook and @Crawley_Jobs_UK on Twitter). If you live in an area covered by this, you can subscribe to a relevant local jobs alert using whatever form of social media you feel most comfortable with.

Another alternative is to use a change detection service such as ChangeDetection (www.changedetection.com). Using change detection is basically asking a computer to keep an eye on a particular website or webpage for you. When that website changes, you get sent a notification. This is particularly useful for monitoring employers' websites so that you can spot when a new job has been advertised.

Alerts are a vital part of the online career toolkit. Ensuring that key information is sent directly to you means that you don't have to remember to go and look for it every week. Receiving alerts can also help to keep you focused on your career building by regularly reminding you that there are opportunities out there.

Networks: How can I get other people to help me find things?

Does social media replace the need to go to conferences?

Conferences and meetings have always been a key place to build networks and get useful information. However, they have some big downsides: they are expensive and infrequent. Social media now allows you to stay in constant contact with your network. It also allows you to set the agenda by asking questions, in a way that was difficult in traditional conferences.

However, don't write off conferences altogether. It can be really useful to actually meet people and to have some dedicated time to think and learn. Conference attendance can be effectively combined with the use of social media to grow and maintain your professional network (see Chapter 4).

'Search' is about finding the information that you are looking for, and alerts are about making sure you don't miss that information. Using your networks to help you find information provides a back-up to these methods and also serves two other purposes.

1. **Happenstance discovery.** People in your network will sometimes send you information that you weren't looking for, but which you still find useful. So if your cousin sends you a job opportunity at her office, you may consider it even if you never would have thought of applying for that job.
2. **Prioritisation.** Your network can help you to prioritise. This is particularly the case where a number of people advise you to look at the same thing. If they all think it is worth looking at, you should probably consider looking at it as well. Most social media works on this basis: the more people *like* something the more prominently it appears in your feed.

We will discuss the process of identifying and building a network in more detail in Chapter 4. So, in this section we will focus on how you can use a network to ensure that you get sent the best information.

In thinking about how to use your network as a source of information it is useful to learn a little bit of network theory. The sociologist Mark Granovetter[vii] makes a really useful distinction between the people in your network with whom you have strong ties and those with whom you have weak ties. Strong ties are to those people who you spend a lot of time with – your family, close friends and immediate work colleagues. You see them a lot and probably share a lot in common with them. In the context of career building, your strong ties can provide you with a lot of support and solidarity: *'Bob, would you look over my CV for me?'*; *'Jane, can I talk to you about a problem I've got at work?'*, etc.

It is important to have close friends and strong ties, but they have some limitations in terms of providing you with information. The problem with strong ties is that they know all the same people that you know, they typically watch the same TV programmes, listen to the same records, read the same newspapers and work in the same industry as you. They are just like you, which is why you like them so much, but because of this they don't know very much that you don't know. What is more, your closest colleagues are also more likely to be competing with you. So, while you may love Bob and Jane, don't be surprised if when they hear about a fantastic opportunity that any of the three of you could get, they keep it to themselves. Therefore, as sources of information, your strong ties are not as useful as you might think.

On the other hand, your weak ties are more useful than you probably imagined: your cousin who lives a few hundred miles away, your old boss, that person you met at a conference a few years ago. These people are all weak ties. They are typically less like you, they read, watch and listen to different things, work in different industries and live in different places from you. Because of this, your weak ties are likely to hear different information from you and less likely to be competing for the same opportunities. They can be an information goldmine.

You want to try and get this email as often as you can.

Hi Fiona

Haven't seen you for ages; I hope all is well.

My company is recruiting a new widget specialist and you just popped into my mind. I remember years ago when we were at college you were always mad on widgets. Are you still in that business?

Let me know if you are interested and I'll pass your details on. If not, we really should get a coffee some time.

Speak soon

Paul

So both strong ties and weak ties are important for career building, but weak ties are particularly important as sources of information.

How can I get good information out of my network?

■ Audit your network. Make sure you know all your connections, and think about who are your strong ties and who are your weak ties.

- Stay in touch. Make sure that you hold on to the contacts you have. Tools such as LinkedIn, Facebook and Twitter are really good for this purpose. They allow you to hold on to weak ties with minimal effort.
- Think about what information you want and where it might come from. If you have decided that you want to work as a lawyer, you need to make sure that there are some lawyers in your network. This may lead you towards some strategic networking (see Chapter 4).
- Tell (some) people what you are looking for. If you are looking for a new job, there are probably people that you can't tell about this, e.g. your boss. However, the more informed people are about what you are looking for, the better information they will provide you with. So, find subtle (or not so subtle) ways to signal what you are interested in to as many people in your network as appropriate.
- Give as well as receive. As a member of a network you need to be a contributor not just a taker. You should try to spot opportunities for other people and provide them with useful information. If you do this, they will notice it and return the favour.

How can I make the most of the information I gather?

So far we've been focusing on how to get information, but as you become a brilliant searcher, sign yourself up for hundreds of alerts and have your whole network researching career information for you, you may discover that you end up in information overload.

Information overload is a feature of the internet age. There is so much information available that it becomes impossible to read it, sort through it and make decisions about what to do with it. One response is to shout 'NO MORE!' and to stop finding any information. Another is to simply give up on making any career decisions, overwhelmed by the information tsunami.

These responses are understandable, but they are not very useful in helping you to advance your career.

A better approach is to develop some strategies for managing information. There are a host of different ways to do this, but here are a few ideas.

- **Allocate some time for sorting through stuff each day or week.** Try not to look at every new piece of information when it arrives. Instead, find half an hour a day or an hour or two each week to work through what has come in. Grouping information in this way will give you more perspective on what is really useful and stop you getting distracted every time a job advert drops into your inbox. If you find that you can't deal with this information in the time you have set aside, consider whether you should narrow your focus.
- **Be clear about what you are actually looking for.** Searching for career opportunities can become a bit addictive. It is easy to convince yourself that somewhere out there is a fantastic opportunity and to waste hours searching for it. However, if you aren't willing to move to Alaska you need to be quick to delete opportunities that are based there.
- **Start scanning and skimming emails and webpages rather than reading them.** Scanning is when you look across some text to find a particular word that you are looking for. So if you want a job as a manager and don't see the words *manage* or *manager* anywhere, you can probably delete it. Skimming is when you read some information quickly to get the gist of it. It might be at this point that you realise that the job is in Alaska or Peru and press the delete button.
- **Use bookmarking services to give you a shortlist of information sources.** There are lots of ways to keep a list of useful sites. Most browsers offer a way to bookmark or to favourite things that you want to return to. Alternatives include social bookmarking sites such as Digg (www.digg.com) or Pinterest (www.uk.pinterest.com). Create yourself a list relevant to your career search and then just check those sites.
- **Assess the usefulness of your information sources.** We'll be looking at how to evaluate the information you find online in Chapter 3, but it is worth regularly asking yourself the question, 'How much time do I spend wading through irrelevant stuff from this source and is it worth it for the number of really useful things that are occasionally buried in there?'

IN A NUTSHELL

Information is a vital part of your career building. Draw together as much relevant information as you can using search, alerts and networks. In general, look for sites and individuals who relate as closely to your career objectives as possible. However, be aware of the value that 'weak links' can offer by passing you information that you haven't seen before. Once you have developed your capacity to source useful career information, you also need to think about how to manage it to avoid information overload.

3 THE INTERNET IS A JUNGLE – BE A CRITICAL THINKER

With so much information out there, you can't rely on all of it to be accurate and up to date. You need to develop the skills of critically evaluating the information you find.

In this chapter we outline a number of ways in which information you find online might turn out to be unreliable, unhelpful or even damaging. We will equip you with a range of tools and helpful habits to increase your chances of sorting the good from the bad. And the great thing is, many of these tools don't just apply to online information. You can use them to evaluate information you get from your Uncle Bernard's best friend's brother as well.

This chapter will cover:

■ spotting and dealing with various types of bad information

■ protecting yourself from fraud and deception

■ sifting useful facts from unhelpful opinions

■ distinguishing between good and bad information.

Avoiding the dangers in the undergrowth

There is no doubt that the advent of the internet has meant that it is much easier to find all kinds of information. Gone are the days when you might spend hours trying to rack your brains to remember the name of that star of an early '90s sit-com who has just turned up in a soap opera. Now, you can instantly look it up.

The development of the social web, where virtually anyone can set up a blog or post updates to social media, means that it is also easier for lots of people to share information as well as to find it. If, for example, you have a personal fascination with the history of the canal infrastructure of the Thames Valley, it is possible to share your knowledge with anyone anywhere in the world who may share that interest. All kinds of obscure knowledge, that at one time only resided in the heads and notebooks of individuals, is now available to all.

In career terms, the internet has made it possible to access information on opportunities, occupations and organisations that it would have taken several trips to specialist libraries to obtain previously.

All of this information means that the internet has become a complex and ever-changing ecosystem within which you can forage for food to satisfy your knowledge needs. But, as with any natural environment, there are potential dangers that might harm the unwary explorer.

One potential pitfall of this international openness is that information and advice that only applies in one country can be read and misinterpreted by job-seekers in other countries. For example, recruiters in different countries often have very different expectations about what should go on a CV or résumé and how it should be structured. When you add to this the fact that, even within one country, different industries may have different rules for putting together a CV, the potential for confusion is considerable.

But there is an even darker side to this openness. Not everyone who publishes information on the internet is acting out of altruistic motives. There are a few who are actively trying to deceive and others who may promote misinformation either intentionally or accidentally.

In the previous chapter we discussed ways to tap into the rich source of information that is available out there. In this chapter we will focus on how to avoid information that may be misleading or downright harmful.

CASE STUDY

Joe has been gathering up a huge amount of information about jobs that he is interested in. He has amassed loads of articles with taglines such as '10 surefire ways to get your dream job'. The only problem is that all of this information seems to pull him in different directions. Some tell him to stalk prospective employers, while others tell him to play it cool. Some say that qualifications are everything and others that they don't really matter. Even on something as straightforward as writing a CV there are differences of opinion. Some say include a photo; others claim that this makes you look vain. What to do? Information is supposed to answer your questions but it only seems to create more.

Joe is initially tempted to just ignore all of this information. If the experts can't even agree then what use are they. But then someone tells him about the CRAAP test (see later in this chapter). Using the CRAAP test Joe thinks about the currency, relevance, authority, accuracy and purpose of the information. He finds that this framework helps him to pare down his pile of advice. Once he has thrown out all of the old, unreliable stuff that has been written by unqualified ranters in other countries and focuses on the quality information about his industry, it all starts to make sense. Of course not all of the experts agree, but they at least seem to be going in the same direction. He ends up with a few solid job-hunting tips and some good leads for landing his next job.

Bad information

The first step in protecting yourself against bad information is to understand the various types of bad information and the people who create them.

- The predatory and the parasitical.
- The manipulative and the misleading.

- The skewed and the subjective.
- The outdated and the obsolete.
- The incoherent and the incomplete.

The predatory and the parasitical

In 2010 a gang of fraudsters posted fake advertisements for jobs on the free classifieds site Gumtree. They claimed to be recruiting for positions at the Harrods department store. When candidates responded to the advert, they received an email that appeared to come from a reputable recruitment agency asking them to download an application pack. The pack contained malicious software which installed itself on their computers and stole their online banking details. The gang used these details to remove over £1 million from people's accounts. This particular gang was caught and jailed in 2013, but there are numerous examples of similar scams tempting job-hunters into applying for attractive positions in the hope of bettering their lives only to find that they have been cheated out of their savings or to receive bills for credit cards they never owned.

At the extreme end of the bad information you may find on the internet are the fraudulent schemes in which someone is deliberately providing false information in order to cause you harm. A relatively common scam is to advertise a non-existent job in order to achieve one or more of the following:

- get your email address so that you can be sent mountains of spam communication
- make you phone a premium-rate number for information or to have an 'interview'
- persuade you to hand over a 'fee' for unnecessary training or police checks
- charge you for arranging insurance or visas for overseas work
- send you a fake cheque then ask you to send back commission on the money you will never receive
- obtain your bank details so they can clear out your accounts
- steal your identity so that they can do various criminal things in your name.

Job-hunters between the ages of 18 and 25 are most likely to fall victim to an online recruitment fraud according to 2014 figures from the City of London Police's National Fraud Intelligence Bureau. The most successful scams aimed to steal about £100 from each victim. However, the average loss per victim from all recruitment scams is around £4,000, meaning that some people are losing a lot more money as a result of this criminal activity.

The Recruitment Industry Counter-Fraud Forum was launched in 2008 and works with a number of organisations, including the Metropolitan Police, to combat criminal activities linked to the recruitment industry. Their website, SAFERjobs (www.safer-jobs.com), contains a wealth of advice on how to avoid becoming a victim of recruitment-related fraud. According to Keith Rosser, the Chair of SAFERjobs, they receive notifications of around £85,000 worth of fraud each month. He comments, *'One of the biggest issues is around job boards and the (often unintentional) use of fake ads. Many job boards are "aggregators", which means they collect job ads from a number of other vacancy websites, and so fake ads can replicate themselves online.'*

Ten tips to protect yourself from online recruitment scams

1. **Be suspicious of any job that looks too good to be true.** For example, if it appears that anyone can apply. Most vacancies will require particular skills, qualifications or experience. If the ad says 'no experience necessary', think again. This could be a sign that they want as many people as possible to respond to increase their chances of finding a victim.
2. **Be suspicious of adverts that encourage you to apply immediately.** Scammers often try to get you to act quickly without giving you time to think. Most reputable vacancies will have fixed recruitment deadlines unless they are in high-turnover areas such as telesales and call centres.
3. **Check with the company where you will be employed.** If an advert claims to be for a job with a particular company, go directly to the organisation's website (don't follow a link in an advert or email) and see if the vacancy is there. If in doubt, call and ask them.
4. **Check links and email addresses.** So-called phishing scams attempt to trick you into visiting a spoof site and entering your login details. They may use web addresses that look very similar to the real site, but there will be subtle differences.

5. **Research the agency.** It is easy to check who owns a web address by using the WHOIS service (www.nominet.co.uk/whois) and to look for information about agencies in the Companies House register (www.gov.uk/get-information-about-a-company).

6. **Beware of poor spelling and grammar.** This can often be the sign of a hastily concocted scam.

7. **Don't just communicate with recruitment agents by email or text.** Try to meet them in person or ask them to phone you. If they are reluctant and give excuses, then be on your guard. Don't phone them in case it is a premium-rate phone scam.

8. **Don't download attachments or allow software to be installed on your computer.** They may be a way for criminals to get malicious programmes on your computer which can steal your passwords and bank details.

9. **Don't hand over money.** Legitimate recruitment agencies charge the employers not the candidates. If you are asked for administration fees or to pay for record checks, the alarm bells should start ringing. If you are asked to pay for training or police checks, tell them you will provide this yourself and bring in evidence.

10. **Don't hand over your personal details.** This also applies to your CV. This would include: date of birth, full postal address, passport number, driving licence number, National Insurance number, credit card or bank account numbers, your weight, height, hair colour, eye colour, marital status, number of children or any other personal information that is not relevant to employment.

For more information on how to avoid recruitment scams and to keep yourself safe online, see the following resources.

- SAFERjobs – www.safer-jobs.com
- Get Safe Online – www.getsafeonline.org
- Action Fraud – www.actionfraud.police.uk

The manipulative and the misleading

You may also find information that is designed to manipulate you and encourage you to behave in ways that are in the interests of the author of the information rather than yourself. This information may not be harmful in the way that the predatory and parasitical information is, but it is certainly not going to do you any good. The main issues that you'll come across in this category are non-existent vacancies and misleading adverts.

Non-existent vacancies

Imagine that you see an appealing vacancy on a recruitment agency site. As with most agency-advertised positions, it doesn't give details of the company but the job itself looks genuine, bearing none of the hallmarks of the scam adverts listed above. You contact the agency only to be told that that particular vacancy has just been filled. However, they expect to have a number of similar vacancies very soon and you can receive details if you register and submit your CV. Disappointingly, those promised opportunities never seem to materialise.

There have been cases of unscrupulous recruitment agencies using fake adverts to encourage job-seekers to register with them. There are a number of reasons why they might do this. Sometimes agencies will market themselves to employers based on the number of people they have on their books. If you want to fill a position quickly, having thousands of potential applicants readily available can be reassuring. Alternatively, a dodgy recruitment agency may just want you for your contacts. They may use your referees and previous employers as business leads, approaching them behind your back to sell the agency's services.

The Recruitment and Employment Confederation (REC), the Association of Professional Staffing Companies (APSCo) and The Employment Agents Movement (TEAM) are all organisations that represent recruitment agencies. Part of their role is to ensure that the reputation of the industry is not damaged by unscrupulous practitioners. Member agencies have to sign up to a code of conduct. For example, the REC Code of Professional Practice (www.rec. uk.com/code) contains the following obligations:

> *In the course of representing a work seeker or client a member shall not knowingly make a false or inaccurate statement, fail to disclose a material fact, or make a representation as to future matters without having reasonable grounds for making it.*

Members must adhere to principles of truth in advertising and will only advertise positions, through any medium, for which they have documented permission to recruit.

In addition, recruitment agencies are bound by the Conduct of Employment Agencies and Employment Businesses Regulations 2003, which stipulates that an agency must have *'information about the specific position of all types to which the advertisement relates'* and it must have the authority to issue the advertisement.

All three organisations provide a searchable database of member agencies so you can check out any agencies that are advertising. You can also use the databases to find reputable agencies that deal with jobs in your sector and location.

Misleading adverts

Some job vacancies make exaggerated or misleading claims about the position advertised. Just as it can be tempting for job applicants to over-hype their achievements on their CVs, a recruiter trying to fill a not particularly exciting role may indulge in a certain amount of exaggeration or intentional ambiguity.

In the UK, the Advertising Standards Authority (ASA) monitors the integrity of all types of advertising, including job vacancies. They administer and enforce the UK Advertising Codes written by the Committees of Advertising Practice. The codes have a number of stipulations about misleading information in job adverts.

- They must distinguish between employment opportunities and self-employed business opportunities (such as franchises where you buy the resources to generate your own income).
- They must relate to genuine vacancies.
- They should not ask potential employees to pay for information.
- They must not misrepresent living and working conditions.
- They must make precise representations of potential earnings, including whether that income is salary only, commission only or a combination of the two.
- They must distinguish clearly between temporary and permanent work.

There are further rules relating to advertised business opportunities and home-working schemes.

- They must clearly state the nature and conditions of the work.
- They may only include figures on potential earnings if this can be substantiated by the experience of existing workers.
- They must make clear any financial outlay that is necessary.

Finally, there are restrictions on the advertising of training opportunities.

- They must not give misleading impressions about the potential for employment after training.
- They must explain what is required to be accepted on the course.
- They must make clear the cost and duration of the course and any other factors that might influence your decision to undertake the training.

With any advertised job, feel free to contact the agency or employer and ask for more details on any of these areas before spending time applying.

Most employers do comply with these rules. However, the rulings section of the ASA website (www.asa.org.uk/Rulings) contains a database of decisions on whether particular organisations' attempts to recruit fell short of these standards. They also have a list of uncooperative online advertisers who have failed to comply with ASA rulings.

There are a number of sites where you can check up on recruitment agencies or advertisers or complain about bad practices.

- Recruitment and Employment Confederation (REC) – www.rec.uk.com
- Association of Professional Staffing Companies (APSCo) – www.apsco.org
- The Employment Agents Movement (TEAM) – www.jobsatteam.com
- Advertising Standards Authority (ASA) – www.asa.org.uk

The skewed and the subjective

So far we've looked at examples where people are deliberately trying to mislead you. However, there are lots of cases where the truth is a matter of opinion. In these cases it is usually a good idea to draw on as many perspectives as possible and to try to remain aware of why the people who you are listening to are telling you their information.

Employer review sites

A number of sites now exist on which it is possible to read reviews of employers by other people in the same way that you can read other buyers' reviews of products purchased on Amazon, and other travellers' reviews of hotels on TripAdvisor. Sites such as Glassdoor (www.glassdoor.com/ Reviews), Vault (www.vault.com), TheJobCrowd (www.thejobcrowd.com) and RateMyPlacement (www.ratemyplacement.co.uk) allow current and former employees to rate and write reviews of organisations. This is a potentially useful source of information which might help you to decide whether you want to work for an organisation – but can you trust what you read?

Because postings are usually anonymous, this obviously provides an opportunity for disgruntled ex-employees to vent their frustrations or competitor organisations to bad-mouth their rivals. However, there's also the possibility of unscrupulous HR departments swamping the sites with fake positive reviews to cancel out any less-than-flattering comments.

It is also worth noting that most of these sites generate income from advertising by recruiters. Employers are unlikely to advertise on sites where they have lots of negative reviews.

Five tips to filter out the fake and the useless on online reviews

1. **Pay less attention to the one-star and five-star reviews.** These are most likely to be people with an axe to grind or people with a vested interest in supporting the organisation. The two- to four-star reviews are more likely to provide a balanced set of pros and cons that will help you.
2. **Dismiss reviews with spelling and grammatical mistakes.** Someone who cannot construct a correct sentence probably shouldn't be trusted to form a constructive opinion.
3. **Look for an agenda.** Think about why the individual has bothered to post a review. Does it look like they are trying to promote an alternative

---

employer at the expense of the one they are criticising? Do they sound like an uncritical cheerleader for the company?

4. **Look for patterns and themes across a range of reviewers.** If a number of different people make the same claims about an organisation, take note. However, be wary if you spot a number of different reviewers using exactly the same phrases.

5. **Pay attention to the specifics.** The more specific and verifiable details a reviewer gives in their comments, the more time you should give to that particular review. Ignore very generic criticism or praise.

Obviously, bias isn't just a problem for online reviews. Even if you talk to a current or former employee of an organisation in person, you can't be sure you're getting a balanced picture. Never base your decision entirely on the opinions of other people (especially if they are anonymous). However, do make a note of any questions or concerns and see if you can get more information about those issues from other sources.

If you have genuine concerns over something you have read about an organisation you are applying to, then you could pose a question about it to an organisational representative at some point during the recruitment process. If the thought of doing that worries you, think about this – what it demonstrates is that you have been diligent in researching the organisation, you are being rigorous in verifying the information you discovered and you are being fair-minded in allowing the organisation to respond. If the organisation is not keen to employ a diligent, rigorous and fair-minded candidate, you probably don't want to work for them.

Careers advice blogs

There are countless career blogs offering insights on everything from how to tweak your CV to how to have your perfect dream job. Many of these are excellent repositories of useful advice for job-seekers, but you can't always depend on everything you read.

Careers blogs fall into a number of categories, and understanding which category a particular blog falls into will help you to evaluate the information provided.

■ **The self-referential amateurs and entrepreneurs.**
These are usually people who have had 'successful' careers themselves, quite often involving some kind of internet start-up, and they are keen to share their experience and wisdom with the rest of the world (and possibly get a book deal or raise their profile for their next venture). Their blogs are typically highly personal and frequently have an inspirational tone which reflects the dynamic personality of the author. The advice they give tends to work best if you are very similar to the author (in which case you're probably writing your own blog between start-ups anyway), but it may not be widely applicable.

■ **The self-promoting careers professional.**
Independent career coaches and résumé writers will often write blogs as a shop window for their talents. The advice and information may be good quality but you have to think about the audience at which the blog is targeted. If the coach mainly works with top-level executives then the advice may not be all that helpful for new career entrants, and vice versa.

■ **The value-adding recruitment site.**
Many recruitment sites provide a careers advice blog as a way of attracting job-seekers or employers. Because the aim is to have regularly updated content to keep the site looking fresh and topical, don't expect particularly in-depth analysis or detailed guidance. The quality can also vary considerably, depending on who they get to write the posts – it could be a jobbing careers professional, a freelance writer or just the latest intern.

■ **The out-reaching careers service.**
Many careers services run their own blogs. The quality of these blogs is often high but it is likely to appeal mainly to the group that the careers service is primarily targeted at, e.g. university students or unemployed people. You will have to make a judgement about whether the advice that is given on these sites is relevant to you.

(Please note that all three authors write or have written for careers blogs, so bear that in mind as you evaluate our advice in this area!)

Five tips for evaluating the guidance you get from careers blogs

1. Always check the 'About' section of the blog to find out the background of the author. How relevant is their experience to your needs? What experience do they seem to have in providing careers advice to other people?
2. Work out the intended audience for the blog. Is it you?
3. Think about how much research the author puts into their articles. Do they refer to relevant external resources, such as published articles and reports? Do they interview relevant people in the field? Or is it just a case of 'Here's another great idea from inside my wonderful head!'? Be especially wary of predictions about the future of work.
4. Beware of national differences when applying any advice to your own career – what works in the US may not work in the UK.
5. Always be suspicious of 'clickbait' headlines. If the blog contains a lot of articles such as 'Ten ways of getting a promotion that will surprise you' or 'You won't believe what recruiters really think about your CV', tread cautiously. It may be a sign that the main purpose of these articles is to generate click-throughs to boost their revenue from online advertising.

The outdated and the obsolete

The world of work is rapidly changing. Information can become outdated very quickly. Always check the date. You will usually find the date at the bottom of the page. If information is more than two years old, be wary. If information doesn't have a date on it, be even more wary. One clue can often be found by checking any links on the page. The older the article, the more likely it is to acquire broken and out-of-date links as other websites get updated.

However, it's not just about old articles. There is also the potential problem of new articles that recycle out-of-date information. When assessing someone's comments it is always worth checking to see how direct and up to date their experience is. Are they talking about something that happened to them yesterday or something they heard about possibly happening to someone else several years ago?

The incoherent and the incomplete

Sometimes information is given in good faith and may actually be correct, but that doesn't make it easy to understand. You often have to spend time trying to decode the information that you find online.

Lies, damned lies and statistics

When looking for information on careers and employment, you are almost certain to come across some statistics. It may be the percentage of graduates in non-graduate level work, competition ratios for sought-after roles or league tables for training courses. The use of numbers can create a strong impression that the information being conveyed is accurate and reliable. That's why politicians and journalists are so keen to quote statistics to back up their arguments and make it sound like they know what they are talking about. We've even done it in this chapter.

All these numbers seem to be providing us with hard facts, but how useful are they? Do they really provide you with a coherent picture of the world of work?

In *Making Sense of Statistics*[viii] from the organisation Sense about Science, Nigel Hawkes highlights the potentially ambiguous nature of statistics by quoting three different figures for the gap in earnings between men and women in 2010. The Office for National Statistics (ONS) claimed it was 12.8%; the Government Equalities Office (GEO) declared it was 23%; and the Equality and Human Rights Commission (EHRC) argued that it was 17.1%. The difference arises from the different ways in which the figure is calculated. The ONS and EHRC use the same data but use a different measure of average salary to make the comparison. The GEO includes different people (part-time workers) in their sample.

This just goes to show that it can be dangerous to take numerical information at face value. It is always worth trying to understand the way those figures were produced. This book isn't the place for lessons in basic statistics, although some of the resources will provide that if you want it.

In his 2010 House of Commons briefing paper, *Statistical literacy guide: How to spot spin and inappropriate use of statistics*,[ix] Paul Bolton gives three essential questions to ask yourself when looking at statistics:

1. **Compared to what?** What information is being used, how was it gathered and what is it being compared to? How big was the sample size? What was included in the measure and what was left out?
2. **Since when?** If you are looking at changes in particular measures (such as unemployment), what time period are you looking at? Were there any conditions in that time period (such as a recession) that might skew the data?
3. **Says who?** Does the person quoting the statistics have a particular point of view that they want to push? Who created the information in the first place? Do the conclusions follow logically from the data?

The following sites have guides to understanding and evaluating statistical information:

- www.statisticshowto.com – this website contains a basic introduction to statistical terms
- www.fullfact.org – this website analyses the use of figures by politicians and other influential people.

The incomplete nature of information

All information is incomplete. The larger and more complex a topic is, the more it becomes impossible to know everything about it. Even the most detailed written description of a job will probably miss out hundreds of things that one day of experience in that role will make you aware of. Even if you have several years of experience in a role, you cannot know that an equivalent role elsewhere will be exactly the same, and it's unlikely that you will be able to predict how that role will change in a few years.

Get used to it. You will never have all the information you need to make perfect decisions. But it can help to know in what ways the information that you do have is incomplete. In simple terms, information can be incomplete in breadth and incomplete in depth.

- **Incomplete in breadth.** This is information that doesn't give enough of the wider picture. We are better able to evaluate the value of something if we are able to compare it against something else. For example, we might think the working hours of a particular role in the financial sector don't look too bad compared to other roles in that sector, but they may still be pretty awful compared to the hours in other sectors. It is a natural tendency to try to narrow down your search as quickly as possible or to only look for information that relates to the options you are already interested in. However, doing some broader research across a range of different employment sectors can provide a better understanding of how your chosen career areas fit into the bigger picture.

■ **Incomplete in depth.** This is information that doesn't provide enough detail or is too generalised. A classic example is the job description. Even if there is a long and detailed list of responsibilities, a lack of information about the amount of time you might spend on each activity means that you don't really know what the job will be like.

The more information we have on a topic, the less likely we are to notice the gaps in what we do have.

Five questions to help you to maintain awareness of the incompleteness of any information you acquire

1. Do I know how typical this is? How do I know I haven't stumbled upon an unusual example?
2. How confident would I be in comparing this career option (or this employer) against similar roles in this sector and roles in other sectors?
3. Can I articulate what I don't know about this? Where are the gaps in my knowledge?
4. How much of my understanding of this job is based on facts I have uncovered and to what extent am I filling in the blanks with assumptions?
5. How many pages would I be able to fill if I wrote down everything I know about this career option, this job or this employer?

Interrogating information – the CRAAP test

If you are going to base decisions you make about your career or your job-hunting on information you obtain online (or from any other source), it is worth getting into the habit of asking a few essential questions about that information.

The following questions are based on the CRAAP test[x] produced by the Meriam Library at California State University. CRAAP stands for Currency, Relevance, Authority, Accuracy, And Purpose.

Currency
Is the information up to date?

- When was it written and when was it posted?
- Has it been updated since publication?
- What time period does it refer to?
- If the information is old, does it still apply?
- Is it possible to find more up-to-date information?
- How likely is this information to change over time?

Relevance
Is the information relevant to you?

- Does the information apply to the career options you are considering?
- Does the information apply in your location? (It can be dangerous to apply US job advice in the UK market.)
- Is it aimed at you or does it mainly apply to people in very different situations or different stages in their careers?
- Does it actually help you to make a decision or is it just making you worry about something you cannot do anything about?

Authority
Where does the information come from?

- Who wrote this?
- Are they writing on behalf of an organisation or just representing themselves?
- Does the website URL reveal anything about the author or the organisation (e.g. .co.uk, .com, .org, .org.uk)?
- What credentials or expertise do they or the people they quote have in the subject?
- What else can you find out about them?
- What else have they written about?
- Can you contact the authors to ask questions?

Accuracy
Can you assess the reliability of the content?

- Do they make a distinction between fact and opinion?
- What evidence is presented and how much do they depend on evidence?
- Is the evidence statistical or anecdotal?
- Do they provide original sources so that you can check the evidence for yourself?
- Can you find similar information from other sources?
- Do they provide a balanced view, pointing out potential weaknesses in the evidence?
- Are there spelling or grammatical errors?

Purpose
Why does this information exist?

- What was their intention in writing it – to inform, to entertain, to influence, to sell?
- Are they trying to be provocative or controversial?
- How open are they about their intentions?
- How one-sided or emotional is the language and tone?
- Do they present different points of view?

Evaluating information on Wikipedia

Wikipedia has become one of the most used sources of information. Rather than having a team of nominated experts to write the entries, anyone who feels they know about a subject can contribute. On the plus side, this means that Wikipedia articles can bring together the collective knowledge of a range of people. On the minus side, it opens up the possibility of people with a particular agenda adding one-sided or inaccurate information to articles. Aside from flagging potentially controversial articles with a warning banner and allowing you to review the history of edits, Wikipedia publishes its own guide to evaluating Wikipedia articles (https://upload.wikimedia.org/wikipedia/

commons/5/52/Evaluating_Wikipedia_brochure.pdf); here are a few tips from that guide to help you to evaluate information from a range of sources.

- **Lack of cohesion or completeness.** If the introductory paragraph doesn't present a complete overview of the topic, or doesn't match the rest of the text, it may indicate an incomplete or piecemeal article.
- **Value-based opinions rather than neutral facts.** A sign of this might be the use of superlative adjectives such as 'best', 'most influential' or 'leading' rather than concrete comparative data.
- **Generalised and unsourced evidence.** Look out for general words, such as 'some' or 'many'. Beware of generalisations hidden in the passive voice: 'they are considered to be …' as opposed to verifiable sources such as '*Business Week* described them as …'
- **Disproportionate weight.** If certain aspects of a topic are covered in more depth than others, or more space is spent on promoting or criticising a particular viewpoint, this could indicate a biased article.
- **Lack of reference to credible external sources.** A good article will provide external links where you can verify the facts presented.

IN A NUTSHELL

When you are exploring the vast resources of the internet, make sure you are well equipped for the expedition. While there is a lot of very useful advice and information available online, you may come across some things that are at best unhelpful and at worst potentially harmful.

It is sensible to ensure that you are familiar with the most obvious warning signs of unreliable information so that you can more easily spot fake vacancies, inaccurate data and poor advice. You should also develop the habit of critically evaluating any information you come across by always asking important questions about reliability, and never relying on just one source.

4 NETWORKS ARE VITAL – BE AN EFFECTIVE CONNECTOR

This chapter will explain who can help you develop your career and how to get them on your side. It will show you how to use the internet to make new contacts and to ensure that the contacts that you already have help you in moving your career forward. It will introduce some of the key technologies such as Twitter and LinkedIn, and show you how to make the most of them; as well as how to combine online and face-to-face networking to get the best of both worlds.

This chapter will cover:

- effective networking

- using online tools to improve your networks

- combining face-to-face networking with online networking

- managing your network.

Is who you know more important than what you know?

We've all heard the phrase 'It's not what you know, it's who you know.' A lot of the time we use this phrase to vent our frustrations when something doesn't work out – for example, when you know that you are the best candidate for promotion but you lost out to someone who was dating the boss's daughter or who went to school with the CEO. This kind of situation can be frustrating, but if we are careful we can use effective networking to help our careers.

Human beings are social animals. We like to spend time with people we know and we often pass on useful information and opportunities to these people. Researchers have demonstrated that there is a strong relationship between the number of people you know and your salary, your chances of being promoted and your overall happiness.[xi]

Who you know matters. It isn't as important as what you know, but you can't ignore the importance of meeting people and maintaining relationships with them if you want to be successful in your career.

CASE STUDY

Diana has been spending a lot of time online talking to people. Lots of people know her, but she isn't really sure how best to make this work for her career. She decides to audit her online activity and think about who she spends time talking to and what she talks about when she is online.

After spending a day taking some notes on her online activities, Diana is surprised at what she finds. She spends a lot of time talking to her old university friends and exchanging jokes and pictures. She also spends a lot of time on LinkedIn talking about work. But she notices that she tends to always talk to the same few people (mainly people from her old workplace). She also has to admit that she tends to spend more time asking questions than answering them. She's not sure that the image she is portraying is right.

Diana resolves to investigate some new sites and to broaden her network. She also decides to think more carefully about how she comes across and try to establish herself as one of the 'go to' people in her field.

What is the point of networking?

Networking is useful to you both in your career and your wider life. If you want someone to fix your television you probably start by asking around your friends, colleagues and neighbours. If someone else has had a similar problem, they can probably link you up to someone who can help. This works in exactly the same way for your career. Networks can help you to access information, advice and support that can help to make you more effective at your job and better at spotting opportunities to progress.

Seven reasons why you should view networking as essential for your career

1. **Information.** You can gain useful information about how different careers and companies work and hear about opportunities.
2. **Inspiration.** Other people's stories can be inspiring and give you new insights on your own life and career.
3. **Learning.** Through interacting with other people you can learn new skills and approaches to questions that you find challenging.
4. **Perspective.** Networking brings you into contact with people who have different perspectives on the world. Accessing a diverse range of ideas and perspectives can be useful when you are trying to make decisions or solve problems.
5. **Support.** Networks provide ways for you to give and receive support and encouragement.
6. **Profile.** Participating in a network can raise your profile and help you to build your reputation.
7. **Patronage.** You have the opportunity to help others through your network. This is worth doing in its own right but will also increase your standing with other members of the network.

If you emphasise only one of these networking goals then you are more likely to be disappointed by your attempts at networking. If you are alert to the potential for all of these benefits, you're more likely to bring something useful away from every networking encounter. You are also more likely to see the possibility for mutual benefit in any connection.

Five steps to online networking

1. **Think carefully about who you want to network with.** It is better to focus on communities than to focus on individuals. So, it is useful to decide that you want to network with people who work in the pharmaceutical industry, but less useful to decide that you want to meet the CEO of AstraZeneca. Once you have joined a community it will be easier for you to make contact with specific individuals within it.
2. **Research this community.** Identify a few prominent and less prominent individuals within the community that you are interested in. Research them online and identify which websites and social media sites they are using – are they discussing things on Twitter, LinkedIn, Instagram or some other site? Look at who they are talking with and use this to increase your understanding of who is in the network.
3. **Create a profile.** Once you have identified where other members of your community are having their conversations it is time to set up a profile on the relevant site. You should ensure that your profile clearly states what you are interested in professionally.
4. **Lurk.** Once you have created a profile, spend some time watching how conversations work in your community. Are they formal or informal? Is there disagreement or unity? How often do people post? What kinds of things do they post about?
5. **Participate.** Once you've done some research you can start to participate. Online networking is all about participation. Depending on the site, you may be able to start just by liking/retweeting something that someone else has posted. But pretty soon you are going to need to start posting for yourself. Good things to post include answers to other people's questions, questions of your own and interesting bits of information that you've found. Ease yourself in carefully and think about how others are seeing you.

How can I be an effective networker?

Networking describes a process of making, maintaining and managing professional connections. Effective networkers are able to meet new people and keep in touch with them. They are also good at making sure that they are particularly close to the ones who are really useful to their career. Some people are uncomfortable with networking, they feel that it is just 'using people' and that it can interfere with real friendships and relationships. However, the first three principles of effective networking mean that you should feel good about networking with people.

1. **Reciprocity.** Reciprocity is all about give and take. No one likes people who are always doing all of the taking. If all you ever hear from someone is *'Can you help me?'* or *'I need a favour'*, it probably won't be long before you stop answering your phone to them. Effective networkers are generous and give their time and advice to others. Because they do that, people are willing to support them when they ask for help in return.

2. **Equity.** We all know people who only want to talk to the most important person in the room. When you meet people like this you can often feel as if you are being sized up and dismissed. These desperate social climbers are pretty easy to spot and often get punished for their bad behaviour. It is much more effective to be nice to people, to be interested in them and to treat everyone with respect. The people you meet may offer a wide range of ideas and insights that might be helpful to your career. What is more, they may be future friends or colleagues. It is also always worth remembering that you never know who the person you are talking to knows. Someone may be low in the pecking order but still be a trusted adviser (or husband or cousin) of the woman at the top.

3. **Authenticity.** When you meet someone new it is important to show them the best side of yourself. But there is no point in pretending to be someone that you aren't. Putting on a fake accent, pretending that you are interested in opera when you aren't or telling outright lies about where you went to school or university are all VERY BAD ideas. People are amazingly good at spotting a fake and will often punish you for your attempted deception. The ability of people to spot a fake extends to the online networking that you do. Online it is very easy to check out any misleading information you share. If people spot you lying they will lose trust in you very quickly.

Being honest, generous and decent are huge benefits in effective networking. But that isn't the whole story. Effective networkers can be good guys but they also need to be well planned and clear about what they are trying to achieve. The next three principles of networking highlight this.

4. **Strategy.** Effective networkers think about who they are trying to network with and why. Just meeting lots of people and chatting with them won't help your career. If you want to be a successful lawyer why are you spending all of your time hanging out with doctors? Your time is limited so you need to make sure that you are spending it wisely, going to the right events and following the right people online.
5. **Tenacity.** There is no point in just meeting someone once and then losing touch. Networking is all about maintaining relationships (that is why reciprocity is so important). So good networkers seek contact with people, follow up once they've met someone and then keep in touch. This all takes time, but it is worth it.
6. **Evaluation.** Networks have a tendency to grow and grow. You might think that it is great to have 6,000 Facebook friends but do you even remember who all of these people are? If you want your network to be effective you have to devote time to the people in it. These should be people with whom you share interests and where the relationships have the potential to help each other forward in your careers. Sometimes this means moving on from old networks and prioritising some interactions over others.

All six of these principles of networking are important. You will need to keep them in mind whether you are networking face to face or online.

What is the point of networking online?

The internet offers us lots of tools that help us to build and maintain networks. Online networking has a lot of advantages over face-to-face networking.

Five key advantages of networking online

1. It is easier to find and contact people online than face to face. You don't have to wait until you are in the same room.
2. It is possible to maintain a greater number of contacts at the same time. Sending an email is a lot quicker than meeting someone for a coffee.
3. It is easier to keep track of your contacts. This includes keeping people's contact details using sites such as LinkedIn, but also includes keeping an eye on what people are doing through their activities on social media.
4. You can build networks with people all across the world (although you should be careful that doing this actually serves your career).
5. You can ask for help and receive it in real time.

However, it is also important to remember that face-to-face networking still has a place. It is easier to build deeper relationships face to face and also easier to make an impression on someone who you have actually met. Later in this chapter we will talk about how you can best combine online and face-to-face networking, but first let's get comfortable with networking online.

Isn't online networking just for people who can't cope with real social situations?

The stereotype of the 'computer geek' still persists despite the fact that almost all of us use computers every day. This much maligned character spends his time in a darkened room squinting at his computer screen and never sees the light of day. He has lots of online acquaintances but has never met any of them in real life. He is living in a 'virtual' world which compensates for his lack of success in the real world.

While we've all met people like this, the distinction between the virtual and real world is getting less and less. If you look around when you are on a train, in a business meeting or even in a night club you'll see that

---

people are constantly connecting to the internet. If you lock yourself out
of these online discussions it might be you who is sitting in the dark!

Online networking actually requires just as much social skill as face-to-face
networking if you want to do it properly; these are different social skills, but
they are still social skills. FOR EXAMPLE, TYPING IN CAPITALS ALL THE TIME
WILL CONVINCE PEOPLE THAT YOU ARE CRAZY, AGGRESSIVE OR BOTH. It
is important to watch how other people interact online, just as you would if you
were networking face to face, otherwise it may look like it is you who can't cope
with social situations.

Is online networking better for some sectors than others?

Depending on where you work and what you are interested in, you are likely
to find different levels of interest in online networking. People who work in the
computer industry are undoubtedly better served in this respect than people
whose job means they are rarely on a computer. However, computers are
gradually penetrating all industries, so it is worth looking around.

Five online professional communities that might surprise you

1. Arbtalk (www.arbtalk.co.uk). You might imagine that tree surgeons
   spend all of their time up trees, but they still find time to participate
   in this online forum for arborists.
2. Society for Underwater Technology (www.facebook.com/SUT.org/
   timeline). Despite being underwater for much of their working lives, this
   international group still manages to maintain a lively Facebook group.
3. Institute for Outdoor Learning (www.linkedin.com/company/
   institute-for-outdoor-learning?trk=fc_badge). This organisation
   serves outdoor educators and currently boasts over 2,000
   subscribers to its LinkedIn page.

4. The busking project (www.busk.co/blog). This blog provides information about and for buskers.
5. Shoe Repairer Info (www.shoerepairer.info). This web forum provides information for all things related to the shoe repair industry.

Increasingly, the internet is everywhere and a part of how almost all occupations do their work. However, each sector is unique and is likely to have its own websites, social networks and forums. Working out which ones apply to you is critical and will require research and time. Searching online is useful, but you should also talk about this with your colleagues. It may be that someone at the desk across from you is spending their lunchtime building their career online. They may be able to show you around the sites that they use and introduce you to some key contacts.

A growing trend is the development of bespoke professional networks that are aimed at a particular profession.

Five bespoke online professional networks

1. Kaggle (www.kaggle.com) is a professional network for data scientists.
2. Muckrack (www.muckrack.com) is a site designed to link up PR and marketing professionals to journalists.
3. Rallypoint (www.rallypoint.com) is a professional network aimed at the military and the defence industry.
4. Research Gate (www.researchgate.net) is a professional network for academics and researchers.
5. The Staff Canteen (www.thestaffcanteen.com) is a professional network for restaurant staff.

Whatever field you work in you are likely to be able to find an online community that will be relevant to your field. However, you should be careful. Just because someone has set up a website it doesn't mean that most people in your field are using that site. This is why it is important to start with research and work out the sites that the people you want to network with are already using.

What is the best tool to build my network?

The tool that you use to build your networks should be chosen with your network in mind. The key question is: what are other people in my field using? However, there are also different types of networking that different types of tools facilitate.

Networking type	What it means	Making it work	What tool to use
Focused networking	Networking to achieve a particular goal, e.g. getting into a particular industry or building your reputation in a specific field.	Network with people who are quite similar to you and share your interest, e.g. they all work in the same industry as you.	Facebook LinkedIn Industry-specific tools
Diffuse networking	Networking to find inspiration and ideas, e.g. to facilitate the early stages of a career change or to stimulate creativity.	Network with people who are different from you and who can offer you new ideas and opportunities.	Twitter

We've already covered some of the online tools that exist to allow you to connect to people in your sector. In general, the tool is far less important than the people. But it is important that we look at the big three social networking tools (Facebook, LinkedIn and Twitter) as well as a few other general professional networking sites.

Facebook

Facebook is the biggest social networking site out there. Given what we've already said about going where the rest of your community is, you may be tempted to think that Facebook is the best place to go. However, there are a couple of things to consider before you make a beeline for Facebook.

■ Facebook is first and foremost a SOCIAL networking site. People share pictures of their nights out, children's birthdays and holidays. Even if you find members of your professional community on Facebook, they may not want to give you access to this kind of personal material about themselves.

■ Where professional communities do use Facebook, you will need to be careful about how this spills over into your social network. It can be difficult to switch from discussing your Aunt Gertrude's birthday with your mum to discussing the latest developments in electrical engineering with your professional community. Your Facebook friends will inevitably find one or other of these more interesting.

This is not to say that it is wrong to use Facebook for professional networking. But there are some dangers in trying to use the site in this way, particularly if you are already using the site for other reasons.

LinkedIn

LinkedIn is the leading professional networking site. It is designed to facilitate professional networking. Key features of the site that help you to network with other professionals are as follows.

■ A **profile**, which is essentially an online CV. You need to keep this up to date, adding new jobs, qualifications and experience as you go.

■ **Connections**, which allow you to link with other professionals and maintain contact more easily.

■ **Groups**, which provide discussion fora for professionals with shared interests. There are an enormous range of LinkedIn groups covering almost every profession and sector. They range from anaesthesia professionals to zoo-aquarium professionals, with everything in between.

■ **Messages**, which allow you to send private (email-type) communications to your connections.

■ **Updates, photos and posts**, which allow you to share information with your connections or the general public.

■ **Prompts of various kinds**, which encourage you to interact with people in your network. Typical prompts might ask you to congratulate someone on a new job, identify a skill that you believe someone in your network has or provide a comment on something that someone has done.

LinkedIn offers you a lot of ways to interact with people in your network. However, it limits your interactions with those people who are outside of your network. It is easiest to talk to people who are directly connected to you (one degree of separation), more difficult to talk to those who are connected to your contacts (two or three degrees of separation) and more difficult still to talk to those who are four degrees or more away from you.

Six degrees of separation

Six degrees of separation is the theory that we are all connected to everyone else in the world by no more than six steps. The idea is that we could all be introduced to anyone else in the world through a series of introductions by a friend of a friend (of a friend and so on).

So I know (1) John and he knows (2) Sally (who works for an airline). Sally knows (3) Quinten who is a member of cabin crew in first class. He regularly chats to (4) Louie who is an international economist who often flies between London, New York and Washington. Louie was at university with (5) Scarlet who is now a political adviser to (6) Barack Obama. It seems that I am only six degrees of separation away from the most powerful man in the world.

Social media sites such as LinkedIn are based on this kind of logic. If you build your network you can eventually connect with everyone who might be of use to you in your career.

In essence, this means that LinkedIn works best once you've got a reasonably high number of connections. More connections provide you with more information, more opportunity to talk to people and importantly a larger network who can link you up to their friends and colleagues.

You should build up your LinkedIn connections gradually, but it is good to aim to get up to about 150 fairly quickly.

Five ways to get connected to people on LinkedIn

You can manage your Connections on LinkedIn with the **Connections** menu at the top of the screen. If you choose **Connections>>Add Connections** you will be offered a range of options to help you find people who you can connect to.

All LinkedIn screenshots used with permission.

1. Start by connecting LinkedIn to your email contacts book. By doing this you can send a connection request to everyone with whom you already interact via email. Assuming that most of the people who are in your email contact book know you well, you should just be able to inform them that you are now on LinkedIn and ask them to connect with you if they also use the site.
2. Use the search facility to find some LinkedIn groups relevant to your areas of interest. Once you get to know some of the key players in each of these groups you can ask them to connect to you. When you are inviting people in this way, be sure to send a personalised message to each contact, perhaps commenting on something that they've said in the group.
3. Use the **Connections>>Find Alumni** option to find people with whom you went to school or university. Again, use a personalised message when you make contact through this approach. For example: 'Hi, I don't know if you remember me, but we were at university together. We now seem to be working in the same field, so I thought I'd make contact.'
4. Use the LinkedIn search facility to allow you to find other people you know. As long as these people are no more than three degrees of separation from you, you will be able to connect to them. Again, send them a personalised message when you connect.
5. Click on the **Connections** link at the top of the **Connections** menu. LinkedIn will then display new people for you to connect with based on the people that you are already connected to.

When you are making connections on LinkedIn (or any other site) you should think carefully about whether this is someone who you actually want to be connected to. If you don't know them or can't see how their interests would connect with yours, it is probably best not to connect.

Twitter

Twitter is a much simpler site than LinkedIn. While LinkedIn offers you the opportunity to network in a range of different ways, Twitter only really allows you to **follow** people and to send and receive short messages.

Twitter has become an important part of the media, entertainment and politics. It frequently breaks news stories before the conventional media. Many celebrities and politicians have Twitter accounts and will broadcast information and interact with the wider population through it.

When you first set up a Twitter account you will need to follow some people. Following someone allows you to see their posts immediately.

Five career and business experts who you could follow on Twitter

Richard Branson	@richardbranson	Businessman and philanthropist.
Chrystia Freeland	@cafreeland	Digital editor, Thomson Reuters – a good source of news and comment.
Sheena Iyengar	@Sheena_Iyengar	Author of *The Art of Choosing*,[xii] which offers food for thought for those making career choices.
Dan Schawbel	@DanSchawbel	Personal branding expert.
Lindsey Pollak	@lindseypollak	Career and workplace expert.

Of course, you can also follow a whole load of other people ranging from Kim Kardashian West (@KimKardashian) to Barack Obama (@BarackObama). Modesty *almost* prevents us from highlighting the fact that you can also follow the three authors of this book: Tristram Hooley (@pigironjoe); David Winter (@davidawinter); and Jim Bright (@DrJimBright).

Once you have followed some people their tweets will start appearing in your Twitter timeline.

Following celebrities can be fun, but it is of limited value for your career. In order to use Twitter effectively for your career you need to follow people who are relevant to your career interests.

Five ways to follow the right people on Twitter

1. **Start by looking for people you know.** Use the search facility to find people who you know (or suspect) are already on Twitter.
2. **Look at who the people you know are talking to.** Follow these people if they look relevant.
3. **Decide who are the most interesting or influential people that you follow.** Now have a look at who they are following. Follow these people if they look relevant. You can see a list of who people follow (**Following**) and who they are followed by (**Followers**) on their Twitter profile page.
4. **Look at the #hashtags that people are using.** If they are relevant to your interests, click on them and see who else is posting to this hashtag. For example, if you are a teacher you might find that other teachers who you follow are using #teacherchat to discuss all things teaching. Anyone using this hashtag might be of interest to you. Follow them if they look relevant.
5. **Search for keywords that are relevant to your area of interest.** See who is using these words and then follow them.

You should aim to follow at least 150 people on Twitter. Once you get beyond about 1,000 people you may find that it is getting a bit too noisy and you might want to cut down. You need enough people to get good information but not so many that you lose track of who everyone is.

What is a #hashtag?

A hashtag is a convention on Twitter that enables people to group messages together to allow a conversation to happen. Clicking on the hashtag brings up a page with all of the messages that use that hashtag.

Hashtags use the # symbol to turn a word into a #hashtag (e.g. #simple, #noproblem #easytodo). Hashtags can't have any spaces, so people usually join words together to form hashtags (e.g. #nospaces, #using_underscores or #UsingCapitals). You can't use a hyphen in a hashtag. Anyone can make up a hashtag: all you need to do is add a # to a word. However, sometimes you might find that someone else has already used that hashtag for something else, so it is worth searching before you launch a new hashtag.

Popular television programmes, such as *Strictly Come Dancing*, are now using hashtags – #strictly – to allow viewers to have a common conversation, even though they don't all know each other. Groups of people who work in similar fields might use hashtags like #engineering, #macuser or #socialworker to allow them to talk to each other.

Hashtags such as #jobs and #vacancies are also often used to highlight new opportunities that are available.

Twitter allows you to post a short message (up to 140 characters) and read the messages that other people post. So, if you wrote *'I'm eating my breakfast in St Pancras station'*, the message would be broadcast to everyone who follows you.

Note: Twitter is essentially public, so anyone can see everything that you post. This means that you should be careful about what you post. Assume that anyone that you are talking about will see the message that you post.

Twitter also allows you to reply to other people's messages (reply) or to repeat the message to the people who follow you (retweeting). Retweeting is important because it allows you to pass on to others information that you have found useful in your networking. Retweeting is one way to keep in touch with your network. Twitter allows you to add a comment or an additional message when you retweet.

How do I get people to follow me/ connect with me?

Networking is a two-way process. Effective networkers are good listeners, but they are also good contributors. When you start networking online it is probably best to focus on working out who to follow and understanding how your network works. However, you don't want to be a wallflower all of your life, and it is important to start contributing. People will only notice that you exist if you have something to say.

But I've got nothing to say!

We are used to spending most of our lives listening to others. When we watch television, go to the cinema or attend a lecture our role is to be listeners while someone cleverer and more important does the talking. Social media turns this on its head – it only works because people all contribute to the conversation. When you first start using it this can be strange and scary.

Lots of people feel that they have nothing to say and that no one would be interested in hearing from them. This is never true. Everyone has some experiences that are different and unique. Sharing what you think or an experience that you have had might prompt someone else to think about something differently. Even if you genuinely know nothing at all, you can still ask questions.

Of course, there is a balance to be struck. Say nothing at all and no one will know that you are there – you won't really be networking at all. On the other hand, constantly sharing your unsubstantiated opinions might lead people to see you as a blabbermouth. In general, try to make short and considered contributions and try to avoid being the most prolific poster in your network.

See Chapter 5 for further discussion on how to communicate effectively online.

Five tips to ensure that people follow you

1. **Post regularly.** You won't become hugely influential if you only post once. Key influencers work at it, adding content and interacting with people every day. Be patient – your influence will be built over years and not overnight.
2. **Be interesting.** Keep posts about your breakfast to a minimum. Think about what information your network would really like to hear about and post that. If you post interesting material then other people will want to pass it on and your reputation will grow.
3. **Be topical.** Notice what is going on in the world around you. If you have got something interesting to say about the current hot topic then you are more likely to get noticed and have people engage with you.
4. **Interact with other people.** Networking is about building relationships with other people. The more you are taking part in conversations with people, replying to them, commenting on their posts and liking what they post, the more likely you are to be able to become part of a network. Interacting with key influencers is a good way to become an influencer yourself.
5. **Be generous.** Acknowledge other people who make good points and pass on the interesting things that they post. It is much easier to spot someone else making a brilliant point than to come up with one yourself. Use this to your advantage and become a good editor and talent spotter for your network.

How can I combine online networking with face-to-face networking?

So far we've been focusing on online networking. However, we live in a blended world where online and offline lives frequently mix. Online networking doesn't replace face-to-face networking – it supplements and enhances it.

It is possible to combine online networking and face-to-face networking in three main ways.

1. **Offline to online.** When you meet someone, make sure that you follow up with them afterwards. Sending an email is a great start: *'It was really nice to meet you the other day …'*. But connecting on social media is even better because it makes a longer-term connection that isn't dependent on you writing to each other all the time. Many people have their social media addresses on their business cards these days, but if they don't then Google them when you get back to your desk. Once you find the sites where they seem to be active for business, add them to your network.

2. **Online to offline.** It is increasingly easy to get to know people online before you ever meet them. The authors of this book met online engaging in arguments, debates and information-sharing over Twitter and LinkedIn. We then continued that connection by meeting up and having a drink together. Obviously it won't be possible to meet all of the people you interact with online, but it is useful to meet with some of the key people when you can. Meeting up helps to cement your relationship and can help you to have a better understanding of how to interact with them online. Conferences that you are both attending offer really good opportunities for this. Another good opportunity is if you are travelling to the town or country where they live. Let them know that you'll be in town and offer to buy them a coffee.

3. **Blended.** An increasing number of events encourage the use of social media (usually Twitter) at the event. The idea of this is that you can be attending a large lecture delivered by a *sage on the stage* and at the same time be interacting with other people also at the lecture. When this works well, people discuss and enhance the main presentation by providing links, resources and alternative viewpoints while the speaker is talking. When it works badly, people can just forget about the speaker altogether and chat. Engaging in this kind of blended networking can be a bit tricky to start with, but it is worth persisting with as it can be a very good way to start engaging with people at conferences.

What if the organisation/individual I'm interested in doesn't have a social media presence?

Not everyone is a social media enthusiast. Once you've read this book you will be an expert online networker; however, you will find that other people's enthusiasm for new technologies varies. It is great to be

---

enthusiastic about social media, but try not to be too pushy! Let people discover it for themselves.

The key thing about networking is to go to the places where you can find people from your network and to talk to them in the way that they are comfortable with. Increasingly, that will be online, but online networking is just a means to an end. If you end up having to meet some key people at conferences and over coffee rather than on Twitter then so be it!

How can I get rid of the annoying people in my network?

Online networks have a tendency to grow and grow. In the past, when you moved jobs or left a particular field you would see your old colleagues less and gradually lose touch with many of them. With social media, once we make contact with someone they stay with us forever.

As your network grows, you will find that it becomes increasingly useful. Having lots of different people, from lots of different places, will give you a wide range of useful information. However, eventually you are likely to hit a tipping point. You've now got so many people in your network that the useless information is outweighing the useful information. You've got to get rid of some people!

Networks are like plants – they need to be carefully nurtured if they are going to grow. But they also need to be pruned when they get too big. Cutting out the people who you no longer share any interests with will improve your experience of networking. Depending on the site you are using, there are different ways to achieve this. You may need to unfollow people altogether or you may be able to choose not to see what they post unless they mention you directly. On some sites you can set up a priority list of the people who are most useful to you.

The key thing to remember is that you haven't got time to be connected to everyone in the world. At some point you need to kick a few people out to make room for some new people.

Five people you should kick out of your network

1. People who never contribute anything.
2. People who you can't even remember.
3. People who bore you or only post things that you aren't interested in.
4. People who get involved in extended flame wars (arguments).
5. People who abuse other people (trolls and haters).

One thing to be careful of is removing people just because you disagree with them. It is good to have a diversity of views in your network.

Haters, trolls and flaming

There is a lot of bad behaviour in online networks. You should avoid behaving badly yourself (I'm sure you never would!) and think carefully about whether you should remove others who behave badly from your network. Key kinds of bad behaviour include the following.

Haters are people who express hatred for someone (usually a public figure online). Online hate speech can often be violent and disturbing. Dump haters if you find them in your network.

Trolls are people who seek to attract attention by making provocative comments. That person who always disagrees or argues with you for no reason is a troll. Life is too short to interact with them.

Flaming is having extended arguments online. We've probably all flamed from time to time. Passions can get raised online. If you spot yourself or someone else flaming, try to calm down. When you are in the middle of a flame war it seems really important to win the argument – when you watch someone else doing it, they just look crazy.

IN A NUTSHELL

The internet offers you a huge opportunity for networking with others. It doesn't replace face-to-face networking, but it can supplement and enhance it. Effective networkers think carefully about the networks that they want to join and then participate in these networks enthusiastically and positively. At the heart of networking are good social skills, and it is a good principle to not do anything online that you wouldn't do face to face.

Networks are built slowly and need to be carefully managed. You need to think about how to get people into your network, but you also need to be careful that your network doesn't get too big.

Networking takes time, but it is worth it. An effective networker gets better information and opportunities than anyone else, they always have supporters to call on and they often have more fun along the way. It's good to talk!

5 INTERACTION IS IMPORTANT – BE A PERCEPTIVE COMMUNICATOR

The internet is all about communication, but the most effective way to communicate will depend on who you are communicating with, what you want to achieve and the nature of the tools you are using. Make sure your communication is honed to perfection in order to avoid some of the common pitfalls of online interaction.

In this chapter we will help you to think about how to communicate effectively online to advance your career. We will give you useful tips for learning the ground rules of any new social media environment. We will also give you practical strategies to get people's attention, manage online conversations and nurture helpful online relationships.

This chapter will cover:

■ the benefits and pitfalls of interacting online

■ key principles for effective online communication

■ some common online communication mistakes and how to avoid them.

Why communicate online?

Communicating online has many advantages over communicating in the world of flesh and blood. It's relatively easy to find and make contact with large numbers of people. It's quick – in some cases you can obtain or provide responses almost instantaneously. In addition, since much online communication is written, you get a chance to review and reconsider your words before unleashing them on the world.

These advantages can also be disadvantages. Because finding people online requires less effort than finding people offline, you can assume that making contact and interacting with them requires less effort too. Similarly, since you can get and give instant responses, you can fall into the trap of not taking your time to think about what you want to ask or say. Because you can hone your written online communication before hitting **Enter**, other people may hold your statements to a higher standard than they would your spoken communication.

The other major disadvantage of online communication is that it is often missing some of the extra information that is available to us in face-to-face communication. Nuances of vocal inflection and body language, which can add subtle shades of meaning to our verbal communication, are often missing in online communication. This missing information can lead to unfortunate misunderstandings when someone interprets your comments in a way you never intended. When I read a comment that you intended as a light-hearted remark, how do I know that I am meant to imagine you saying it with a warm tone to your voice and a cheeky twinkle in your eye?

CASE STUDY

Joe attends a really useful seminar given by Hittesh, who is one of the leading figures in his field. Joe is really excited by the seminar and picks up Hittesh's business card. On the way home from the seminar he types a message into his phone and sends it off to Hittesh.

'That was g8!!! I'd love to connect and get some more advice from you. Can I give you a call sometime next week?'

Hittesh doesn't find the email in his inbox until the middle of the following week; when he is out running seminars he often finds that his email box gets a bit flooded. When he opens Joe's email he is a bit confused as to what it is about and who this person is. He puzzles for a moment and then hits delete.

He also has an email from Diana in his inbox. Diana also attended the same seminar, but she waited until she got home to get in contact with Hittesh. She spent a few minutes researching Hittesh and found that he was active on LinkedIn. She decides that that is the best place to contact him, but she also decides that she needs to do it carefully because she imagines that he will get a lot of emails.

'Dear Mr Gupta, I attended your seminar in Norwich last week and I found it really interesting. I was wondering whether you would be willing to connect with me on LinkedIn. I know you are busy, but I was also wondering whether you could point me to any information on that example you gave about practice in the Netherlands. I thought that was really interesting and I'd like to find out more. Yours, Diana.'

Hittesh picks up Diana's email request and happily accepts her as a connection on LinkedIn. He also responds to her and sends some more information about the example he used. Diana then thanks him and begins to correspond with him further.

Improving your communication skills

A search for *communication skills* in the books section of Amazon produces over 100,000 results. There is a big market for advice on how to communicate better, and plenty of people willing to offer their expertise. Even though we often take the ability for granted, effective communication in the real world requires vast mental resources and years of practice. As a species we've been doing it for millions of years and we still get it wrong quite frequently. We've only been doing online communication for a few decades.

This tendency for us to get it wrong is quite useful. One way to explore how to communicate more effectively online is to look at the common mistakes that people make and to understand why they make them.

Before we do that, let us first go to an unlikely source of inspiration to learn some essential lessons about how to communicate effectively online.

Communication lessons from internet trolls

In the previous chapter we mentioned a group of people you should try to avoid online – trolls (people who deliberately try to make you angry and waste your time). However, before you assign them to the oblivion they deserve, it is possible to learn several important lessons about online communication from the activities of these disruptive misfits.

At first it may seem as if the only thing you can learn from people who insist on throwing abusive comments into online discussions is that there are idiots wherever you go. However, there are more sophisticated species of trolls which use subtler tactics to hook people and draw them into increasingly heated online exchanges. Whether simple or sophisticated, these internet irritants appreciate something about communication that is also understood by the most adept communicators.

One of the most powerful possibilities of communication is that you can trigger an emotional reaction in another person just using your words.

This is important because our emotions drive our behaviours. If you want someone to respond to your attempts at communication, they are more likely to do so if they experience an emotional reaction to what you say. For trolls, the aim is merely to provoke indignation and frustration. These emotions then drive otherwise reasonable people into making rash responses that they may later regret.

There are numerous articles offering advice on how to deal with these online agitators and they all boil down to the same thing: *Do not feed the troll.* The best way to beat a troll is not to give them the reaction they desire. Don't rise to the bait. Ignore them. Despite this advice being repeated over and over, the trolls still manage to get people to fall for their tactics. How do they do it and how could you put these tactics to better uses?

Think about the emotional reactions you want to produce

Trolls are single-minded in the emotional reaction they want to elicit. Whether they are quick-fire abusers or more subtle game players, they are entirely focused on igniting the spark of anger inside their victims.

When communicating online, it is always worth trying to anticipate the potential emotional impact of your comments. At the very least, you might reduce the risk of causing unintended reactions to your remarks. At best, you will increase your chances of having interesting conversations and building mutually beneficial relationships.

When interacting online, it may be possible to provoke various feelings that increase the likelihood of people acting in particular ways towards you. For example, you might stimulate feelings such as:

- curiosity and fascination, so that people take an interest in you
- trust and acceptance, so that people share resources (such as information) with you
- protectiveness and nurturing instincts, so that people help and support you.

You might provoke curiosity by presenting unusual ideas or asking thought-provoking questions. You might generate feelings of trust by drawing attention to areas of common ground or by generously sharing resources with others. You could stir nurturing feelings by highlighting the extent to which you value someone else's wisdom.

Trying to generate emotions such as these can have its dangers. It is all too easy to come across as pretentious or presumptuous or just plain needy. There is, however, one fairly safe emotional outcome that you can aim for in every interaction – affirmation. If you make other people feel appreciated and valued, you greatly increase the chances that they will want to continue communicating with you. There is still a possibility that, if you do it clumsily, you will come across as a sycophantic creep. You can reduce that risk by avoiding generalised praise and making the effort to give specific, positive feedback. If someone shares something that you find interesting or useful, tell them why it meant something to you. If they answer your questions, explain exactly how their answers have helped you. If they talk about their achievements, let them know what that has inspired you to do.

Know your audience and their passions

Trolls choose social media sites where people with strong interests gather together. The more people you have with a passionate interest in a particular topic, the more likely you are to find someone who will react. More sophisticated trolls are also able to anticipate what will get a reaction. Whether it's politics or religion or parenting or cats, they know which issues will aggravate their intended victims.

Take time to get to know the people you are communicating with. The great thing about online communication is that it is often possible to look at how people have reacted to comments in the past, to observe patterns in the things that they respond to or ignore. Of course, instead of finding out what annoys people, you might want to discover what inspires them, intrigues them or excites them.

Nurture engagement

If someone takes a troll's bait, the troll is quick to respond in order to try to reel in their catch. They will try to feed the flames of frustration growing inside their victims. The lesson from this is to ensure that you respond quickly and positively whenever someone engages with you online. It could be something as simple as always remembering to thank someone if they retweeted you, but it goes further than that.

Whenever someone responds to you online, it is worth thinking about how you might turn a one-off transaction into an ongoing conversation. The more you interact with someone, the more you can learn from them and the more they can learn from you. As you build an online presence, you may want to pick and choose who you engage with, but, when you are relatively new, it is worth trying to nurture a conversation from every interaction just to see what works.

One of the best ways to keep a conversation going is to ask questions. Later in this chapter we will discuss how to formulate good questions, but that task is a whole lot easier if you start by taking an interest in the other person. Being interested in other people's perspectives and experiences is one of the most effective safeguards for avoiding communication errors of all kinds.

Common communication errors

Not communicating

There are a great many things that you can just read or watch on the internet. Similarly, there are many advantages in 'lurking', or observing an online interaction between other people without contributing yourself. One benefit of lurking is that you can take time to notice how other people communicate in a particular context and identify the helpful or influential people in a particular community.

However, if that's all you do, you'll be missing out on some of the most beneficial aspects of social media. These come through interacting with people that you might find it difficult to encounter offline.

Many people hold back from getting involved in online interactions because they either believe they have nothing interesting to say or that they might end up saying something they regret.

I have nothing interesting to say

The glib answer to this concern is that if everyone on the internet waited until they had something interesting to say, there would be a lot less online communication. However, even if everyone else is engaged in banal celebrity tittle tattle, while you are using the internet to build your career, you need to be operating at a higher level.

Let's try another approach. Think about someone you know who always says the most interesting, witty or entertaining things. Next, think about someone you most enjoy conversing with regularly and with whom you could talk for hours. Are they the same person? My prediction is that they're probably not. And, here's my next prediction: if you think about the person you enjoy talking to, one of the characteristics of that person is that they seem to be interested in you a lot of the time. Obviously, the ability to make fascinating statements and the trait of being interested in other people are not mutually exclusive but, if you're going to pick one to help you with better communication, pick the latter. **Don't put pressure on yourself to be interest*ing* but do try your very best to be interest*ed*.**

Curiosity is a much safer motivation for communication than a desire to look impressive. If you want to join a conversation, the best thing to do is to think of a question. Later in this chapter we will look at how to ask better questions, but here is one to start you off: 'What do you think about this?'

I might say something stupid

Sticking to asking questions in the early stages of any online interaction will probably keep you reasonably safe from most embarrassment and conflict. However, unless you want to sound like a demented quizmaster, you can't keep asking questions all the time. At some point, you might have to express an opinion on a topic, and that is where the danger can arise. Even in this situation, being in the habit of asking questions can keep you safe. This time you need to ask the questions to yourself.

Questions to ask before you post something online

- If someone already thought of me as a selfish idiot, what is the worst interpretation that they could put on my words?
- What does this statement reveal about me and what do I want it to demonstrate?
- In what ways might a future me regret saying this? How could this come back and bite me?
- Would I want a potential future employer finding this comment just before they interview me?
- If the person I'm addressing this to were sitting in front of me, would I say this?
- What would my saintly grandmother think about me saying this?
- If I say this out loud using the voice of a sulky teenager, a mass murderer or a used car salesperson, how does it sound?

Getting the tone wrong

Humour and emotions

Making funny comments online can be a serious business. Humour is an immensely powerful aspect of communication. It can be used to strengthen a bond between collaborators and it can also be used to hurt and belittle your enemies. A comment that would cause a stranger to slap your face might be a bantering indication of trust and affection to a close friend. It is this double-edged nature of humour that makes it particularly hard to do well online, where many of the non-verbal cues that indicate a comment is not meant to be taken seriously are missing. This is especially true of sarcastic or ironic humour in which the intended meaning of the utterance is often very different from the literal meaning of the words used.

Light-heartedness is not the only emotion that is difficult to convey using text-based communication. One way round this difficulty is to use emoticons or smilies to indicate the emotional intent of a comment. Emoticons were originally combinations of characters that made a picture (often if viewed sideways). Many mobile phone operating systems and social media sites now substitute graphic images, or 'emojis', for these symbols.

Common emoticons and their meanings

:-)	Classic smiley – *one of us just made a humorous comment* or *I'm just happy*
:-D	Big grin – *one of us has been really cheeky*
\:D/	Dancing – *I'm so excited! And I just can't hide it!*
:-(	Sad face – *I'm unhappy, perhaps because you said something that upset me*
:'(or :_(	Crying – *one stage beyond sad face*
</3	Broken heart – *even more devastated*
X-(	Angry – *I'm furious with someone; it might be you*
:-o	Shocked – *I didn't expect that* or *Look how shocked I'm pretending to be*
#-o	Doh! – *someone has been really stupid*
0.o	Confused – *I'm giving you my best perplexed look*

;-)	Winking – *nuff said!*
>:) or **:>**	Evil grin – *one of us just said something wicked or controversial*
:-7 or **:S**	Sarcastic – *don't take what I just said literally*
:-I	Indifferent or Deadpan or Saying nothing – *basically, I'm hard to read*
:-P	Sticking tongue out – *I'm concentrating very hard* or *I'm blowing a raspberry at you*

The use of such symbols in more formal settings may produce a real-life ☹.

A safer method is to use *intention statements*. These are metacommunications – or communication about the act of communicating. Just like emoticons, they often reveal the underlying emotions and tell the other person how to interpret the words they are linked to.

Some commonly used phrases, such as 'only joking', 'this is probably a stupid question', 'but seriously' or 'don't quote me on this', are metacommunications, as they tell the listener how to receive the accompanying comment. Some intention statements are so overused that they have often come to mean the opposite of what they actually say. 'With the greatest respect' now almost invariably means 'with no respect at all', and 'no offence meant' usually means 'I'm quite aware I've said something offensive, but I'm not prepared to apologise.'

If you are trying to convey something emotionally complex that could easily be misinterpreted, it is worth including more explicit intention statements to compensate for the fact that you cannot communicate this complexity with your tone of voice and body language.

Examples of intention statements

- **'This is a genuine question.'** If you think there's a danger that the other person might think you are attempting to be clever or sarcastic.
- **'What I'm about to say will probably sound a bit controversial/stupid/ flippant/etc.'** If you want people to listen to your full argument rather than just reacting to your first comments.
- **'I may not express this perfectly.'** If you would like people to be patient with your struggle to articulate what you mean.
- **'This might be a bit of a cheeky thing to ask, but ...'** or **'I will completely understand if you say no, but ....'** To preface a request so that you don't sound too presumptuous when asking for a big favour.

Perhaps the best advice when it comes to communicating strong emotions online is: **don't send it, sleep on it**. Write it down, but save it and look at it again in the morning when you have calmed down, and are more able to imagine what impact your communication might have on other people and on yourself.

Jargon and acronyms
Humans use language to facilitate mutual understanding, but we also use it to identify people who belong within our group and those who are outsiders. That's why there are so many different languages and dialects of languages and regional variations in accent and vocabulary. Every profession or hobby develops its own special jargon and ways of communicating. This has the positive purpose of making interactions between insiders more precise and more efficient, while simultaneously achieving the more negative purpose of making it harder for outsiders to join in. Being able to use relevant jargon appropriately can help other members of a group to accept you as one of them.

The internet and mobile phones have generated their very own special jargon in the form of abbreviations. Originally designed to reduce the number of characters used in text communication and early internet message boards, these TLAs (Three Letter Acronyms) are often used to confuse and exclude the n00b ('newbie' – someone unfamiliar with the conventions of a particular internet forum). Such jargon can be wonderful for gaining street cred among your friends, but is probably best avoided in more formal career-related communication.

The best way of dealing with unfamiliar jargon used by other people is to use artless honesty – 'I'm revealing my ignorance here, but what does TLA stand for?' (Note the use of the metacommunication – 'I'm revealing my ignorance here' – to give a tone of slight emotional vulnerability.)

Some internet abbreviations that are also metacommunications

SMH   Shaking My Head – *my disbelief or disapproval is too great to express in mere words*

TBH   To Be Honest – *I no longer have the patience to be polite*

NBD   No Big Deal – *I really don't care* or *I care a lot and I'm being politely sarcastic*

IMHO   In My Humble Opinion – *I dare you to disagree with me*

AFAIK   As Far As I Know – *my awareness of this is limited and I have no intention of researching the issue*

IANAL   I Am Not A Lawyer – *I disclaim any responsibility for what I'm about to say; don't blame me if it's wrong*

JK   Just Kidding – *I just said something potentially offensive and I'm trying to CMA* (Cover My Arse)

NRN   No Reply Necessary – *I'm not interested in any response you may make*

NTL   Nevertheless – *I'm about to contradict myself* or *I'm about to ignore what you just said*

PTMM   Please Tell Me More – *I want you to expand* or *you have already told me too much and I'm being sarcastic again*

DIKU   Do I Know yoU – *why are you bothering me with your unqualified opinion?*

Register and formality

The term 'register' relates to the level of formality of language used in a particular context. In a higher-register setting, one is expected to adhere more strictly to the conventional rules of grammar and spelling. Down the casual end of the register you can get away with things a bit more, 'cos it's not quite so stuffy.

The challenge of application email etiquette

Back in the old days when you printed your CV and cover letter on paper and sent them by post, things were much easier. In the UK there were well established (if somewhat arbitrary) rules about how you structured a letter: 'Dear Mr Weasley ... Yours sincerely' and 'Dear Sir/Madam ... Yours faithfully'.

In the email age, things are more complicated. Do you still use 'Dear', or should it be 'Hi' or 'Hello'? Is 'Yours sincerely' too stuffy, and should you use 'Kind regards', 'Warm regards' or just 'Regards' instead?

In emailed job applications, it is still better to stick to the traditional 'Dear ... Yours' formulation unless you have already had fairly extensive contact with the person you are sending your application to, in which case 'Hi ... Kind regards' is probably acceptable. If you feel the urge to use 'KR' or 'Krgds' (or anything else), only do it with people who are likely to forgive you.

Five bad habits from texting that can damage your communication

1. **i type everything in lower case.** You might create the impression that you don't know where the SHIFT key is or that you are just too lazy to press it.
2. **u.** Do u think u are being charged by the letter for this message or do u only have one finger on ur right hand?
3. **Thankyou** and **thx.** It might happen one day, but so far 'thank' and 'you' have not fused into a single word. 'Thanks' is edging towards the informal, but 'thx' has definitely crossed the line into annoying.

4. **Not using any punctuation however complex your sentence to help clarify your meaning.** For snappy text messages and tweets, punctuation is often unnecessary. Expecting the reader to insert your punctuation for you in longer texts is just rude.
5. **Overdosing on exclamation marks!!!!** Use them sparingly or you risk coming across like an overenthusiastic puppy.

Choosing an appropriate register can become even more complicated when communicating internationally. Many cultures have communication rules linked to showing respect to those who are older, to strangers or to those who have positions of authority. In some cultures it is expected that you will make flattering comments to someone who is of higher status, but do this in a different culture and it looks a lot like slimy sucking up. At the other extreme, addressing a complete stranger as if they are a long-lost close friend can be irritatingly presumptuous.

This is complicated even further by the fact that different industries and professions have different cultural norms for the levels of formality and deference that are expected. You can get a rough idea of what might be expected by observing how people dress in their online photographs. The more formal they are dressed, the more likely it is that they like to be formally addressed. There are exceptions to this. Many scruffy university academics still like to be referred to as 'Professor'. Pay attention to how people sign themselves off in their own communications.

If in doubt, the best option is to start relatively formal, with title and surname, and then ask if you can call them by their given name.

Boasting and self-deprecating
In some cultures it is normal to speak highly of yourself and be open about your abilities and achievements, whereas in other cultures this would be the height of arrogance and bad taste. Conversely, the understated modesty you would display in the latter cultures would be interpreted as symptoms of dangerously low self-esteem in the former.

For any interaction, you need to think not just about how you want to portray yourself, but also about how the other person might interpret your words and actions differently from your intentions because of their background and expectations. The next chapter on building a brand will discuss various ways in which you can create a positive impression online.

Asking the wrong questions

Whether you are trying to investigate potential career options, exploring how a new contact might be able to help you or just gathering more information to boost your chances in a job application, the ability to ask the right questions is vitally important. As we mentioned earlier, asking questions can be a great way to start engaging with other people online – whether you're participating in a LinkedIn group discussion, following people on Twitter or joining a Google Hangout.

Unfortunately, many job-hunters and career explorers waste the opportunities presented to them by asking questions that are not likely to get them the information they need. If you want to increase your chances of success, it's worth spending a bit of time brushing up your question-asking skills.

Open and closed questions

Any question to which you can just reply 'yes' or 'no' is a *closed* question. Examples include:

- Did you enjoy working at PricewaterhouseCoopers?
- Are teamwork skills important in software development?
- Will I be paid for this internship?

Closed questions are great for checking your facts and your assumptions but they don't oblige the other person to provide more information. They might guess that you need more than a 'yes' or 'no' answer but they don't have to give it.

Open questions invite a fuller response and they always start with one of the '5Ws and 1H'.

The 5ws and 1h

- What
- Where
- When
- Who
- Why
- How

Using open questions will get you much more useful information, as you can see from these example questions.

- What did you enjoy about working at PricewaterhouseCoopers?
- When are teamwork skills important in software development?
- How much will I be paid for this internship?

If you want to go a little further, you could try asking pseudo-closed questions. These are structured like a closed question but have an open question embedded within them.

- Could you tell me what you enjoyed about working at PricewaterhouseCoopers?
- Would you be able to expand on when teamwork skills are important in software development?
- Do you mind telling me how much I will be paid for this internship?

Even though they are slightly more cumbersome, they have the advantage of extra politeness because they allow the person being questioned the appearance of autonomy. In theory, they could just say 'yes' or 'no', but a positive response will involve them giving you the information you need.

Chunking up and down
Think about the difference between these three questions:

1. Why are good communication skills important to working in accountancy?
2. How are good communication skills important to working in accountancy?

3. When are good communication skills important to working in accountancy?

The chances are that the first (why) question will lead to a slightly more abstract, conceptual answer about the meaning of communication in accountancy (chunking up) and the third (when) question will prompt slightly more specific, concrete examples of the application of communication (chunking down). The middle option (how) could go either way depending on the person answering the question.

Different people may find one direction of questioning (up or down) easier to respond to than the other. This depends on whether they tend to engage in more abstract or more concrete thinking in relation to the particular subject. Generally, the more expertise that someone has in a particular field, the more they will tend to talk about it in abstract terms.[xiii] If you need an expert to be more concrete, you will need to keep asking 'when' and 'how' questions.

Pay attention to your own tendencies when formulating a question. Is the construction of the question likely to generate the kind of answer you need? Also pay attention to patterns in the way people respond to your questions. If you want people to engage more, ask questions that lead in the direction (up or down) that they seem to be most comfortable heading.

Effort and perspective
It is always worth asking yourself how easy it will be for the other person to answer your questions. Think about how much effort they would have to put in to provide the answer you need.

For example, you might be attracted to working in the film industry. You know it's competitive and will be hard work to get into. Therefore, you want to get an insider's insight into that world to help you decide whether you would enjoy it enough to make the effort worthwhile. Through assiduous networking you manage to find a contact who works in that sector and you ask them, 'What is it like to work in the film industry?'

Oh dear! Just look at all the work you have placed on your poor contact's shoulders! Even assuming you can be more specific and you ask about what it is like to work in particular roles in the film industry, if they are to give you the answer you need, they will still have to:

- make a mental checklist of the various factors that might influence the enjoyment and satisfaction that someone gets from their work
- guess which of those factors are likely to be most relevant and important to you
- recall all of their experiences in the industry that might relate to those factors – and recall what they have heard about other people's experiences
- evaluate those experiences for the emotional impact they might have on you
- find a way of explaining and interpreting those experiences to someone who doesn't yet have the industry vocabulary.

That's a lot of work! This explains why, when you ask this kind of question, you are likely to get fairly trite answers such as 'I've loved every minute of it,' or 'Only think about working here if you are completely mad.'

If you want to obtain high-quality information from people, you have to put a lot of the effort in yourself, either after or before you ask a question.

One approach is to encourage the other person to talk from their own perspective without having to take your needs into account. So, you could ask questions such as:

- What have been the most and least satisfying aspects of working in this role for you?
- What things surprised you most when you started in this field?

This is much easier for the other person as they never have to leave their own frame of reference. However, you will then have to put in the effort of interpreting their answers and working out how much they apply to your situation and your preferences. This could involve finding other people who may have different perspectives so that you can look for similarities and differences in their responses.

Putting the effort in beforehand involves providing the other person with more information to help them enter your frame of reference and answer the question in a way that is helpful to you. So, you could indicate which factors are most important to you by asking questions such as:

■ To what extent would this role suit someone who likes working in teams?
■ How often do you get to decide your own approach to a particular task?

These more specific questions are still easier for your contact to answer than a broad, open question because you have given them clear prompts about the type of information you need.

Choosing the wrong communication channel

It is worth thinking carefully about what communication medium you use. Twitter or instant messaging can be great for interchanging information and resources. It is good for asking questions but, unless the question is fairly simple, it is much less useful for answering them.

The more generous word limits of LinkedIn and Facebook updates give you a better opportunity to express more complex ideas unambiguously. Even so, they are not the place for lengthy discussions as other updates will keep getting in the way of your discussion.

LinkedIn groups, Google+ and dedicated online forums are structured so that more in-depth discussions can develop with specific participants.

The problem with all of these methods is that they are 'asynchronous'. This means that you cannot monitor the other person's reactions as you speak to them. You have to send off your comment and wait to see what response comes back. If you are discussing something more sensitive or you need to gauge the other person's level of enthusiasm, it is worth switching to a voice or video chat service, such as Skype, FaceTime and Google Hangouts. Adding voice and video gives you more information on the other person's state of mind.

The ultimate option is to arrange to meet someone IRL (in real life). This can have great advantages, not just during the face-to-face meeting itself, but also for subsequent online interactions. Having met someone in the flesh, it is much easier to imagine their tone of voice and characteristic body language when you next read their online comments. This means that you are less likely to misunderstand them. Of course, whenever meeting an internet contact for the first time, take sensible precautions, such as meeting in a well-populated public setting. And don't get drunk, or you might find you have committed yourself to writing a book with the people you meet.

Wherever your conversation starts, be prepared to suggest moving the discussion to a more appropriate channel if you start struggling to understand or be understood.

Great communicators use ToM

If you want to increase your powers of communication online and offline, don't just focus on the content of what people say, but also notice the way they say it – and try to imagine what they are thinking and feeling as they say it.

Theory of Mind (ToM) is the ability to infer what is going on in another person's head based on their observable behaviours and reactions. The more you can exercise theory of mind to understand the intentions, motivations, beliefs, etc. of someone who is quite different from you, the more effective you will be as a communicator.

Communicating online is particularly hard because often all you have is the words. Most of the information you would normally use to help you develop a ToM for the other person – their intonation, facial expressions and gestures – are missing. With online communication, you cannot rely on your natural instincts. You have to be more systematic about making inferences about other people's intentions.

Whenever someone makes a comment online, ask yourself the following questions:

- What might have led that person to make that comment?
- What were they feeling when they wrote that?

- How did they expect people to react?
- How many different explanations can I come up with?
- What are the best and worst interpretations I can put on this?
- Am I basing my assumption of their intentions on what my intentions would be if I had written that?

IN A NUTSHELL

The opportunities for engaging with people on the internet are unparalleled, but online conversations can present challenges in addition to those already inherent in face-to-face human communication. Potential blunders and misunderstandings are more likely, so you need to pay more careful attention to the way you communicate.

Communication isn't just about the sharing of information. Emotions play an important part in developing online relationships. Just because they are less obvious in the written word doesn't mean they are not there. Take time to think about how you convey your own feelings and interpret other people's motivations. This may require you to use communicative techniques that you may not use in your day-to-day interactions.

Don't just pay attention to the content of your online communications, but concentrate too on the style. Pick up clues about the most appropriate tone to adopt and be prepared to adapt your approach to suit the circumstances.

6 BUILDING A BRAND – BE A SKILLED STORYTELLER

In this chapter we ask you to think about how others see you online. When you are online, every move you make leaves a trail of information for others to find. These 'digital footprints' can be used as clues by employers and your professional peers to make judgements about your professionalism, your skills and your personality. We argue that you should work to transform this trail of information into a positive online brand. You then need to carefully manage your online brand to ensure that you present the best possible career image to the world.

This chapter will cover:

- what a brand is and how to build it

- getting an effective presence on LinkedIn

- understanding how to write an effective blog

- understanding appropriate content and images to post

- how to create attractive online content that will build your personal brand and advance your career.

Do employers really look at your social media profile when recruiting? Are they allowed to do that?

Yes and yes. Estimates vary from study to study, but it is clear that a growing number of employers are using social media as part of their recruitment processes. It is probably worth assuming that any recruiter you are interested in might look at the information that you've put online. Putting information on social media is like putting up a billboard next to a busy road featuring yourself in your birthday suit. There will be some people that don't see it the first time, but you can bet your life, once aware of it they will make a detour down the road just to have a look. Using the privacy settings provided on social media sites to protect your modesty is like trying to cover up the billboard with a hanky. There will be plenty left for others to look at.

Frankly, if you have to ask the question 'Are they allowed to do that?', you are probably coming at this issue from the wrong starting place. Supposing a recruiter does somehow 'illegally' gather or use information about you derived from social media posts, it would be very hard to prove and, even if you did, the chances of you subsequently landing the job or keeping it would be diminished. Far better to assume that what is out there is fair game for recruiters, and therefore focus on taking down the inappropriate stuff, and ramping up the material that enhances your reputation.

How much time should I spend on social media?

A common mistake for people engaging in social media is to invest a lot of time (and sometimes money) in making a big splash and then not following it up. You see a flurry of activity and then nothing for long periods of time. In contrast, others become almost addicted to various platforms, and the more self-aware among this bunch will take complete breaks from any social media interaction for periods of time. This phenomenon is seen most often in Twitter, with high-profile examples, such as Stephen Fry (@StephenFry and @MrsStephenFry), going cold turkey on Twitter for periods.

Blogs are another area where you will find plenty that start in a burst of enthusiasm and then peter out after a few months. Some bloggers pick too narrow a topic and write themselves into a corner, whereas others become disheartened when their blogs fail to have a major impact within the first month of publication. However, the most successful bloggers, whether it be Belle de Jour (www.belledejour-uk.blogspot.co.uk) or lGuido Fawkes (www.order-order.com), gradually build up a following over months or even years.

Building a social media profile does not have to take a lot of time, but it has to take lots of times. In other words, the key to building a profile is to keep on publishing regularly. Aim for short, sharp and succinct. Aim for a tweet or retweet a day, or a blog of 300 words a week a or twice week, or one or two three-minute YouTube videos, etc. Social media is not set up for long, incredibly well-researched pieces. Do not fall into the trap of endlessly perfecting your blog posts. Remember, the perfect is often the enemy of the good.

Your brand can become closely associated with what you do on social media. This is why it is important to get it right. The comedian Stephen Fry has become closely associated with Twitter and uses it to further his career and the things that he is interested in. As it is likely that you aren't already a celebrity, you will probably need to establish your brand from scratch. One way to do this is to become associated with an interest or area. You might wish to be the person who tweets regularly about exotic ice cream, or comfy office chairs. Whatever the topic, if people learn that there will regularly be something new to read if they follow you, you will find more and more people do just that.

What is an online brand?

A personal brand is the collection of ideas, products, services and reputation that people associate with you. An online brand is a marketing term referring to how a person, product or service is positioned online. For our purposes, you are trying to market your own 'brand'. Your online brand is how you come across on various social media platforms, but it is also important how this brand connects to the real you in the physical world.

If you think of the following brands, what springs to mind?

- Coca Cola®
- McDonalds®
- Nike®

The answer is, of course, junk food for the first two, and exercise for the last one – to counteract the sugar and fats! Seriously, just those names are sufficient to bring to mind soft drinks, fast food or sports gear. We bet you also cannot see those words without bringing to mind the Golden Arches, the Swoosh or the Dynamic Ribbon Device (as Coke's graphic design is officially called). This is a great example of successful branding.

If one of your goals of engaging with social media is to grab the attention of people who can further your career, you will want your name to become synonymous with your knowledge, skills and abilities. You want your readers to connect your name to what you offer in the labour market. So, for instance, we all know that Brian Cox is the astronomer who used to play in a pop band, or that Nigella Lawson is an author, presenter and chef. These people have been very effective in getting us to remember them for what they do as well as who they are. They each have a brand, and you will need to create one for yourself as you build your career online.

What is 'content' and why is it important to an online brand?

So, building a brand is about building positive associations between you and your offerings. So how do we go about this? The answer is content. Content builds your brand.

Content is the stuff you put online. Content includes: tweets, profiles, CVs, blogs, answers, comments, likes, updates, invitations, connections, friends, photos, images, sounds, articles and quiz results. In other words, content is anything that is put in the public domain (and, despite privacy settings, assume everything can find its way into the public domain).

Ten steps to develop your brand

1. **Decide what it is you have to offer.** For instance, you might have a law degree or be an excellent user of Photoshop.
2. **Think about what you want.** For instance, you may want a job as a corporate lawyer or a graphic artist. Thinking about what you want helps you to clarify what content you need to create and who you would like to read it.
3. **Decide who you want to talk to.** It is important to know your audience. What are they looking for? What are their expectations in terms of presentation, customer service, professionalism and expertise? Also consider, what gets your customers interested and excited? For instance, corporate lawyers are likely to expect a corporate and reasonably serious presentation. They will expect ethical behaviour – so, no sharing indiscreet remarks about clients or yourself. They are likely to get excited about legal updates, information about potential clients, stories of lessons learned from the corporate legal world, information about the next big thing in their world, and most importantly how to improve their practice and profitability. Personal interest stories that your readers can use as examples in their own work are also likely to be popular.
4. **Do something.** You will only build your brand by putting yourself and your content out there. It can be frightening at first, but you need to push through that and actually post. Start by being extra careful and cautious, but recognise that practice makes perfect and that you will find each public post easier than the last.
5. **Be consistent and reasonably focused.** Treat your audience with respect. Treat them as though they have paid to come into your theatre and are expecting a good show. This means sticking to a subject area or topic, and not straying too far from this. In the same way, many actors can lose

credibility and our patience when they start pontificating about political matters: your audience doesn't care about your cat, your passion for tiddlywinks or other topics unrelated to your expertise. You may have strong views on the decline in church architecture in the 19th century, but sadly nobody cares if they are there to read about new innovations in trainspotting.

6. **Be careful in your use of different platforms.** If LinkedIn is the formal business meeting, Twitter the business text message, then Facebook is the conference bar, or weekend company event. Although it may be expected that you are more personal and forthcoming on Facebook compared to the other platforms, if you choose to allow potential employers or colleagues access to all three platforms, then it is important that the way you present appears to be shades on a continuum rather than Dr Jekyll and Mr Hyde.

7. **Don't trash your brand.** Many years ago, Gerald Ratner, then chairman of the jewellery company bearing his name, described their best-selling product in a public meeting at the Royal Albert Hall as 'total crap'. The reaction was instantaneous – £500 million wiped off the value of the company that very nearly collapsed, and Ratner himself was sacked within the year. This happened before the time of social media! These days that remark may well have led to an irreversible collapse. Don't do a Gerald on yourself!

8. **Develop a style and stick to it.** Usually, the best style is write as you sound in real life – in other words, try to be authentic. It might take some experimentation to work out which style works for you. For instance, if you are not very funny, leave it to those who are. There are many different 'voices' you could adopt, including: fair-minded; independent; factual; critical; sarcastic; satirical; humorous; up-to-the-minute; a sharer; an originator of ideas; a supporter; a representative; a booster of other initiatives; the insider's perspective; the view from the top; the voice of the masses; the customer; the technical wizard; the helper; the objector; myth buster; taboo breaker; campaigner or the spokesperson for a group. You do not necessarily have to adopt only one voice, but trying to speak in too many different voices is likely to confuse your readers and even alienate some who have come to expect or prefer one of the other voices.

9. **Keep on keeping on.** Your brand will be built slowly across thousands of small acts and conversations. Setting up a LinkedIn profile or a blog is great, but it is only when you start to use this regularly that it really starts to have an impact.

10. **Review how it is going.** There is no point in banging your head against a brick wall. It is important to spend a bit of time thinking about what you are doing that is working. Many social media platforms offer you a range of statistics. Have a look at these and see who is looking at you (and who is not). Are you unexpectedly big in China? Is there a topic that you talk about that everyone seems interested in? Once you find out what things are working, then do more of them.

Isn't an online brand just some overblown marketing hype?

If you are not careful, you can take the concept of 'brand' too far. A brand's strength can also be its weakness. Once a brand becomes closely associated with a particular range of products, it can be hard for the public to accept so-called brand extensions to other products or services. Thinking about 'celebrity' brands, you might not be overly convinced by, for instance, cigarette companies promoting cancer research, or fast food companies promoting diet plans.

Individuals are not baked beans. That is, the problem with the brand idea is that people are more complex than a tin of baked beans. There is more to most of us than a source of nutrition whose consumption makes us unpopular in lifts. For example, it might be great for a while that your brand is associated with providing free information and help to others. However, it could work against you if you subsequently decide to charge for your knowledge and services.

A better strategy might be to develop a so-called 'freemium' service model. This is developing a reputation for providing generic advice for free, but where there is a clear expectation that there are fees for more specialised, advanced, extensive or personalised material.

Equally, if you have a strong reputation as a butcher, you might find it difficult for people to accept you as a serious applicant for a role as a spokesman for animal rights charities or the Vegan Society. A brand can become a straightjacket and lead to us being stereotyped.

Thinking you are a brand, or going over the top with the marketing-speak branding approach, can also lead to the impression that you have delusions of grandeur. If you have never met one of those exceedingly irritating types that talk about themselves in the third person, you are indeed blessed. They have succeeded so well in turning themselves into a product that it has taken on a life of its own, quite separate from the real person. It is an unattractive look.

Using ideas from branding, such as targeting a market and having a consistent approach, look and content, are worthwhile ideas to take on board, but do not go overboard in the process.

The basics – building a LinkedIn profile

LinkedIn is a great place to have an online presence if you wish to interest recruiters. LinkedIn is built around your 'profile'. A profile is essentially an online CV.

Making sure that you exist online

Get onto LinkedIn and create your profile. It is easy to do and starts with navigating to www.linkedin.com. We've already given you a few tips on getting started in LinkedIn in Chapter 4, so you might want to review those before you get going here.

You will be greeted with this screen:

Think carefully about the name you sign up with to ensure it is the name you want to be known by or are best known by. For instance, one of the authors is better known as Jim than James, and this is reflected in his LinkedIn Profile. Remember what we said about brand consistency? To be consistent, ensure you use the name most closely associated with you. This may include previous married surnames – perhaps in parentheses, after the name you prefer now. And don't vary the way you use your name without good reason. Be Jim or James or Jimmy or J, but not all of them at once.

Next you are asked the following:

You can then move on to the screen asking to start building your network.

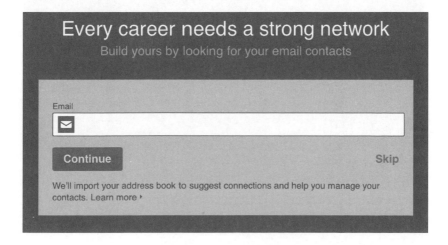

We covered this in more depth in Chapter 4, but the networking aspect of LinkedIn is so important that it is worth saying again. You should think carefully here about whether you want LinkedIn going through your address book and importing all the contacts. You may have an untidy address book, with many out of date or out of favour contacts that you do not want to meet all over again in social media. So, before you choose this option, think carefully.

Then, you are asked to select some channels to receive news updates on your interests.

This is a great way to get involved and see who is who in the zoo. Aim to follow channels that relate to your work or the work you want to get into. There is nothing stopping you following other channels out of pure interest of course!

Now, when you log in you have the bare bones of a profile, and you'll be greeted with the following screen.

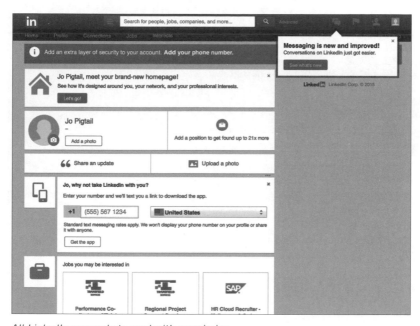

All LinkedIn screenshots used with permission.

This is the time to enrich the profile to generate interest among colleagues and recruiters, to build your brand and to showcase yourself, your knowledge skills and abilities.

Adding a photo is an essential in our opinion.

Photo tips for social media profiles

■ **You must have a photo and it must be an identifiable picture of you.** People will be far less willing to engage with you if you won't even share what you look like.

- **A head and shoulders shot is preferable.** Your face should take up two-thirds of the picture, so it can be seen easily when presented as a small image on a screen.
- **The picture should be current.** Your photo should look like you now – so dump those student pics of you with long hair (even if you were thinner then).
- **You should present a professional image.** Hair and clothes should be appropriate for the kind of work that you are interested in. If in doubt, go smarter than you think you need to.
- **Choose an appropriate background.** Ensure that the background fits your desired workplace and that it is not distracting. If you have books in the shot, replace *Fifty Shades of Grey* with something work appropriate, unless of course your work is ….
- **Smile and look relaxed.** Think of something genuinely amusing while the photo is taken and look directly at the lens. If you are not comfortable smiling, at least go for the Mona Lisa half-smile. In jobs where you want to convey seriousness of purpose, gravitas or power, more than openness or friendliness, an expression of engaged concentration can work. The key is to look relaxed and assured.
- **Make the most of yourself.** A LinkedIn photo isn't a beauty competition. However, you should look at your best. So, comb your hair, put on your make-up, sit up straight and do up your tie. If you have a fuller face or a thicker neck, try turning your neck and looking slightly upwards. You'll be able to find a whole host of other tips about looking good in online photos in magazines and on the internet. However, be careful not to overdo it. There is a fine line between looking good and looking like you are posing for a glamour shot or the cover of your third album.
- **Don't take a selfie.** It is usually pretty easy to spot a selfie. No matter how cleverly you take it, people will usually know. Unfortunately, selfies are associated with vanity and frivolous behaviour.
- **Take more than one photo.** Models and photographers alike know that to get a good shot you often have to take hundreds of pictures. You needn't get carried away, however, taking a few pictures and choosing the best one is always a good strategy.

> ■ **Ask someone else for their opinion.** You are going to live with your
> profile picture for quite a while, so ask for someone else's opinion
> on it before you post.

Next, you should add some positions (former jobs) to your profile. LinkedIn
claims that this increases your chances of being found by 21 times. Also add
your education, as this is claimed to increase your chances of being found by
seven times.

Adding this information is going to take time, but having your CV to hand will
help. For experienced people, you might spend an hour or two entering all your
details. This is time well invested, and you should take care with your profile as
this is your shopfront to the LinkedIn world.

Inviting connections

Once your profile is complete, you need to invite connections. The easiest way
to do this is by allowing LinkedIn to trawl through your email accounts and
address books. Otherwise, you can connect by knowing the email address of
your invitee. Later, once you have been accepted as a member of a LinkedIn
group, you can connect to other group members by inviting them on the basis
of your shared membership.

Respecting connections

It is our experience that LinkedIn members expect any news or promotional
material to be posted in updates or to groups. They DO NOT expect to receive
promotional messages sent directly to them and a list of others. Respect
your connections – they did not sign up to LinkedIn to be on your marketing
database. One of the fastest ways to lose connections, and possibly have your
account suspended, is to get overly eager and market yourself or your services
directly via email.

Joining groups

LinkedIn has a great feature called Groups. These can be found under the
Interests tab on your menu bar. You can browse the different groups, or try
searching for them. Broader search terms will yield more possible groups.
For instance, at the time of writing, a search for 'Chemical' returned 2,062

different groups, whereas a search for 'Chemical Engineering' returned 444 groups. If you have the time, starting broad may yield some groups you hadn't considered.

You can join up to 100 groups. Each group can now have up to 20,000 members. 'Official' LinkedIn groups, such as Recruiter Network, are a lot bigger.

Why join groups?

When joining groups, consider what you are trying to achieve. If you want to connect with recruiters who have jobs in your area, then search for recruiters in groups. The biggest group here is Recruiter Network, which has over 729,900 members at the time of writing. The group welcomes job-hunters and you will get the chance to network with recruiters. Once you are accepted as a member, go into your group settings (under the 'More' menu tab) and check the box to allow 'members of this group to send me messages' option.

- Groups are a great way of establishing connections with other people. If you want to invite someone to connect, sharing the same group membership gives you the right to approach the other person. Without it, you need to know that person's email address.
- Groups are a great way to build your brand, by showcasing your expertise and helpfulness in your posts and interactions with others in the group.
- Groups are a great way to learn from colleagues in your area.

Participating in groups

There are some definite dos and don'ts for new players on LinkedIn groups.

Ten Dos and Don'ts for LinkedIn Groups

1. **Do read the rules.** LinkedIn groups usually publish information in the **About** section of the group saying what the group is about. Sometimes they will have published a detailed set of rules saying what you can and can't post about. Try to respect the purpose for which the group was set up.
2. **Do lurk, listen and learn (at first).** Don't dive in with a contribution until you get a feel for how the groups work.

3. **Do ease yourself in gradually.** Start off by sharing or commenting on other people's posts, before posting your own material. Do it in a respectful and positive way. Look for areas of agreement and common ground. Suggest other resources and provide links if appropriate.

4. **Do be polite.** Manners cost nothing. Being polite and courteous is always a good idea. Being rude and boorish will always be noticed by others (including by people who may not comment on it at the time but will remember for the future).

5. **Do be helpful.** When we talked about networking we covered the idea of reciprocity. This principle of good networking means that it is in your interest to be nice to other people and to help them where you can.

6. **Don't self-promote (very much or very obviously).** LinkedIn groups offer you a huge opportunity to network and build your brand. However, if you just keep banging on about how wonderful you are you will kill the golden goose. It is fine to tell people about things that you are doing (if they are relevant), but try to make sure that they don't shade over into being a hard sell for you, your product or your pet cause.

7. **Don't express your opinion without thinking about it first.** Just 'liking' someone's post can send a signal about your attitudes or affiliations. It is not just negative posts that you need to be careful about. If someone posts a very positive article in praise of a dodgy practice, liking it may seem supportive of the poster but it will also say a lot about your values. So, 'Ten ways to conceal a murder at work' is probably not the ideal post to be liking (no matter how useful you found it!).

8. **Don't post in anger. (Sleep on it.)** Avoid responding immediately to a post that angers you. Get it out of your system. If the response is genuinely unfair and unreasonable, it is likely that somebody else will point it out without you needing to dive in. If it is a point that is reasonable but you disagree with it, consider what you gain and what you lose by trying to have the last word. Remember, 'No comment' is always in the top three best responses you can give.

9. **Don't flame.** Sometimes group discussions can escalate into slanging matches. There is nothing to be gained from encouraging the perpetrators or getting involved. It is best to walk away – do not react and do not get drawn in. Trying to defend yourself by having a go back at someone online rarely looks anything other than ugly. Even interceding to try to calm things can be hazardous. If a reader sees a lot of unprofessional banter and among it is your name, despite

being an innocent party, you will implicitly become associated with unprofessional acts.

10. **Don't overuse humour.** We have all done it: told a joke, only to see the other person look bewildered because they don't get it. That is, if we are lucky. Some of us have, unfortunately, told a joke only to realise we have just terribly offended our friend who we discover too late either has no sense of humour, or really does like Barry Manilow records. On social media this can be 100 times worse. A lot of the subtlety of humour can be lost, and you never know who your audience will be, and what state of mind they will be in when they read your contribution. Make sure that you signpost when you are being humorous by using phrases such as 'only joking!' or 'just kidding'. Humour can also upset those who are particularly passionate or deadly earnest about a topic, and can be interpreted as you not taking it sufficiently seriously. Also, beware of in-jokes between colleagues in public forums – they are likely to alienate those not in on the joke; save such communications for private messages.

Sharing updates

LinkedIn allows you to post status updates. These are seen by all of your contacts unless you change your privacy settings. Be judicious in what you post for status updates.

Ten dos and don'ts of status updates

1. Do post news about your career if it is significant. For example, you might want to tell people about your promotions, awards and exciting projects.
2. Do post links to blog posts on other platforms such as WordPress, Squarespace and Livejournal.
3. Do share interesting posts from others.
4. Do share events you are putting on, or think worthwhile attending.
5. Do share job ads that are relevant to your contacts.
6. Don't send trivial posts about your breakfast.
7. Don't send the same information twice.
8. Don't bombard your connections with updates … one to three or four per day is fine.

---

9. Don't send or share inappropriate material. This could include sharing bad jokes or links to things that you actually disagree with.
10. Don't post or share political or religious material unless you don't mind being labelled for your views. You may feel that you have a duty to speak out, but you need to remember that others may judge you for this.

Skills, endorsements and testimonials

LinkedIn allows you to select up to 50 skills to include on your profile (go to edit profile and scroll down until you come to 'Skills'). This is an important way to get noticed, and LinkedIn claims you are four times as likely to be found if you include skills. Choose your skills carefully with an eye to the kinds of work you want to do in the future and ones that promote your brand. Though it is tempting to select as many skills as possible, this may be counterproductive because of the way endorsements work.

When you connect to another person, they will be asked to endorse the skills you have selected; so, for example, they might be asked does Jo Petersen have skills in the area of sales? The number of times other people have endorsed your skills is displayed next to each skill. It can be best to start off with a relatively small number of skills, as you are more likely to get more endorsements quickly, since each of your contacts is likely to be asked to endorse the same skills. With a larger set of skills, you can end up with a lot of small number endorsements spread across a large number of skills; this looks less impressive.

How do I construct my LinkedIn profile if I'm pursuing different types of jobs?

Change is inevitable. As your career progresses, you will need to change the way you communicate your brand. Sometimes, this is going to happen over a very short period. For example, you might be fed up at work and think, 'If I don't get a promotion I'm going to quit my job and retrain as a teacher.' At this point, you are effectively trying to create two brands at the same time: one as an ambitious executive who is keen to climb the corporate ladder, and the other as an aspiring teacher. This can be tricky.

Ideally, you won't be trying to pursue all of these opportunities in a single week. It is much better to focus on one thing at a time, and to tweak your profile to signal your interest in the new areas that you are focusing on. There are lots of ways you can alter your profile to make yourself a better fit for different jobs. Here are a few tips.

Sex up your headline

One of the easiest ways to alter your profile is to change the 'headline' message in your profile.

Your headline can be a lot more than your job title or the company you work for. Consider instead putting a statement about what you have to offer, what makes you stand out from the crowd. Examples might include:

- 'Head of Corporate Consultancy & Research at The Careers Group – Careers, Professional & Leadership Development'
- 'Professional Chicken-Sexer, with industry awards for both vent and feather sexing'.

Use the keywords the advertisers use

Step 1. Search for a job advert on LinkedIn that is typical of what you are looking for. For instance, see image opposite:

Step 2. Copy the position description and paste it into Wordle (www.wordle. net).

BUILDING A BRAND

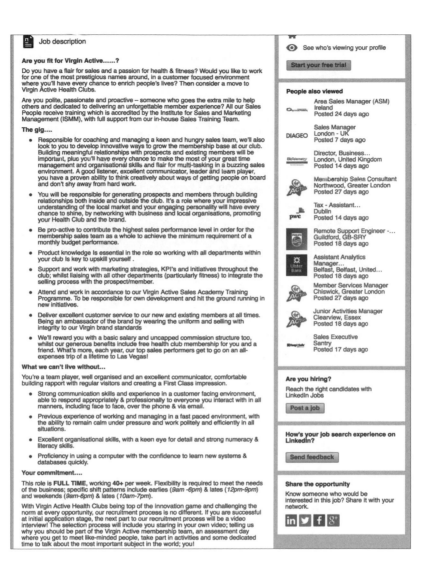

The Wordle has picked out the key words for you! For this job, you can see that frequent words include 'experience', 'skills', 'calm', 'managing' and 'literacy'. These kinds of words help you to understand the kind of language you should use when responding to the job advert. Other words give you more of an idea about the specific skills that they are looking for in this role, such as 'systems', 'computer', 'databases', 'customer' and 'politely'. Wordle just looks at the most frequently used words, so, while you shouldn't rely on it to read the advert for you, it does give you some good insights into what the recruiter thinks is important enough to mention twice and the kind of language they use.

Step 3. Sprinkle these words throughout your profile, in the headline and in your various job descriptions. This will maximise the chances of you coming to the attention of recruiters.

Does having a LinkedIn profile mean I can just sit back and wait for people to find me?

If you are not seriously looking to build a network or find a job, then doing nothing is a perfectly reasonable strategy. If you could be subject to awkward questions from your current employers if you were seen to be actively chasing recruiters or contacts at competitors, then the passive (or secretive) approach is for you.

However, if you are free to look, and you want to be seen, then you need to go out and after people. Contribute to groups, send invitations to connect, fine tune your profile to attract recruiters, go in search of the connections that are going to help you achieve your goals. The passive approach is not for you.

Blogging

Writing a regular blog can be an excellent way to develop a profile and brand in social media. Blogs have made superstars out of people from all walks of life, and in some cases bloggers have been so successful that the blog becomes their career, earning a good income from advertising, endorsements and even, subsequently, in-real-life (IRL) public appearances! However, it is worth noting that the number of people who make a living out of blogging is very, very low. A blog is usually a part of your career, rather than the whole of it.

Think of a blog as a little like a diary entry – it is a regular short reflection on a topic or a theme. Obviously, if you are trying to build your brand, a blog on a topic that is relevant to your brand is important. Ask yourself, how can I be useful to other people? What are they going to find informative or entertaining or preferably both?

The seven ingredients of a good blog

- **Say something relevant.** So many blogs are totally pointless. People don't care about your observations on trivial matters. They do, however, want to read material they can relate to, or information that will assist or amuse them.
- **Say something original.** A blog should reflect your opinions and values. If you are merely repeating other people's ideas without adding anything, then readers will quickly give up on your blog and go straight to the horse's mouth. Reposting material from other people is only valuable if you add your take on it. Think about why people might make a beeline for your blog rather than someone else's.
- **Write it succinctly.** Do not waffle or beat about the bush. Blogs that are about 300 words are easy and quick for readers to absorb. It is fine to add even shorter blog posts that are, effectively, just a couple of sentences but that link to something useful. However, once you go much over 1,000 words you are putting a burden on your readers.
- **Write it grammatically and clearly.** A blog is no excuse for sloppy grammar or poor spelling. You might not give an owl's hoot for a possessive apostrophe, but there are owls out there with their eyes on you. Attention to these details shows care and respect for your reader. It is about communicating a clear message. Grammar and clarity is also something that employers care about (a lot!). This also entails structuring your blog logically so that it is easy to follow, memorable and persuasive.
- **Use illustrations.** A picture paints a thousand words. Well-chosen illustrations will make your blog more attractive and memorable.
- **Write it invitingly.** Good blogs aim to engage their readers and encourage comments. Ending your blog with an invitation to share a view or comment will encourage interaction and feedback and may spawn other ideas for a blog.
- **Say it regularly.** Blogs live or die by regular content or a lack of it. Blogging takes time and commitment, some bloggers will spend three or four hours on each post. If you cannot find that time, or your topic is easily exhausted, blogging may not be the best option for you.

Blogging: some popular platforms

Here are some of the most popular blogging platforms. We would recommend WordPress – it is free, easy to use and very popular.

- Blogger: www.blogger.com
- Drupal: www.drupal.com
- Ghost: www.ghost.com
- Joomla: www.joomla.com
- Livejournal: www.livejournal.com
- Squarespace: www.squarespace.com
- Tumblr: www.tumblr.com
- Weebly: www.weebly.com
- WordPress: www.wordpress.com

Blogging: Is there much point blogging/tweeting if nobody reads/follows you?

The blogger's perennial complaint is that they have sweated over their blog for hours, eagerly posted it, and nothing happens. Blogging can feel like repeatedly dropping pennies down an infinitely deep well; unrewarding and a tad pointless.

You need to be realistic about your expectations. In the same way that every group of friends with a garage and a guitar hope to have a number 1 hit, but almost none do, blogging is unlikely to give you the fame of J.K. Rowling. Nevertheless, so many people are doing it these days. The blogs that gain some traction generally have a clearly defined niche. For professionals, this could be a blog that is specific to an area of practice. A very successful series that ran on YouTube was devoted to making film special effects in your backyard (Indie Mogul).

All blogs start with no readers. So, do not despair if nothing much seems to happen in the first few months. Even high-profile bloggers can put out blogs that next to no one reads. Some blogs take off and others take time. Treat each blog as a learning experience, where you are honing your skills. Try to write as elegantly and persuasively whether you have no readers or 1 million readers. Over time, and with some promotion from you by pasting links on other social media sites, readers will come.

However, even if no one ever reads your blog it can still be useful. Thinking about something and writing it down is a really useful learning experience. You will remember the things that you have blogged about and you will become an expert by doing the research that you need to do for your blog. Employers want to employ people who are reflective lifelong learners and a blog provides you with evidence that you are just that.

Stuck for Content

If you are stuck for content, consider getting onto a site called Meddle (www.meddle.it). This is a site that allows you to curate content from other sources on the web. For instance, you can place widgets in your browser that allows you to cut articles from news sites you are reading, and add comments. The beauty of the site is that you can add more than just the 140 characters available to you in Twitter. So, you could use Meddle as a site for a regular blog and commentary on contemporary issues in your area of expertise.

Check out the blogs of people you admire. See how their content varies over time. Do not be afraid to write on the same topics. Spot where they have gaps, or perhaps where you might disagree with something they have written.

A portfolio of your writing/ideas
The best way to have a good idea is to have lots of ideas. Get into the habit of recording ideas as they come to you. A notes app on your phone or voice recorder might be a good way. Some people send texts or emails to themselves. We prefer written records, because it is generally quicker to retrieve the ideas later, rather than having to listen to every recording to

find the one you require. Use 'spare' or boring time – for instance bus and train journeys – to jot down the ideas that come to you. Showers are often great thinking places; you are sufficiently focused on the shower, but the task is not demanding and allows your mind to wander. Make sure you have your recording device near the shower to capture those moments.

If I put my best ideas on my blog, won't people just steal them?
A common fear for bloggers is about sharing information – and with good reason. If you have plans to put out a product or service, then giving away too much information about it in advance could be an invitation to a competitor to steal the idea and steal a march on you. However, for the rest of us, frankly, that fear is overblown. You might be so excited by your idea you are convinced it is gold, but, in fact, it is just an idea. Sharing your idea may help you to get feedback on it, raise the level of interest that you have in it and even attract possible funders. It is clearly a bit of a balancing act. You want to give away enough to get people interested, but not everything.

Some occupations do not lend themselves to sharing everything. For instance, comedians who share their act online put pressure on themselves to make up an entirely new act because a joke heard once is generally enough. A famous comedian, Bob Monkhouse, lamented that when Pavarotti sang 'Nessun Dorma', people didn't heckle with 'heard it', but, sadly, that is the comedian's fate.

If you are concerned that sharing might lessen the impact of your work, or may ultimately undermine you, then clearly do not share everything. There are still ways to share portions of your idea or your work as tasters to engage an audience and build up demand for when you eventually reveal the great idea.

For everyone else, sharing can be a very helpful and powerful way of demonstrating your expertise and building your brand. The more you share, the more content is out there for others to rely upon, the more you develop your influence.

Do I have to be controversial to get noticed and will I damage myself in the process?

One person's controversial is another person's bland and yet another person's gross offence. Put simply, there is no accounting for taste or other people's reactions. It is probably easiest to start off by considering the legal aspect to this because that is relatively clear. There are laws against racial vilification, breaching official secrets, the publication of obscene material, threatening material and defamatory material.

Defamatory material when written is libel (slander is spoken). If your words are likely to cause harm to the reputation or livelihood of another, you may find yourself in hot water. You will generally need to prove that what you said was true, or that you had good reason to believe it was true, and did not act recklessly in publishing. Or, you need to prove that the other party consented to what you wrote.

You may think this is all rather heavy, and not relevant to the average social media user. Think again. Comedian Alan Davies tweeted speculating about the identity of a Tory Party paedophile, and subsequently retweeted a message naming a high-profile Tory. He was sued and settled for £15,000 in damages. Be careful what you put out there, and be careful what you retweet, or otherwise share.

So, assuming we have overcome the legal hurdles, there are other considerations regarding being controversial. Controversialists can be very engaging, even amusing if they do it well, and appear to believe what they say. However, by definition, controversy is polarising. You need to have a very clear idea of why you would want to alienate 50% of your potential audience before you engage in controversial postings and, of course, you need to be very sure your view on whatever the topic happens to be is not likely to change, given the eternal nature of social media posts. .

A common trap to fall into is to claim you are being controversial when, in fact, you are expressing rather mainstream bland views. So, for instance, saying something like 'I am going to be controversial here: I like internet cat videos', will serve only to irritate those whose expectations of some controversy were dashed. You are likely to come across as an attention-grabbing nobody.

If you are working or commenting on an area of specialist knowledge, then controversial views are likely to be challenged with evidence. If you are going to express controversial views in this arena, you need to have some fairly robust and well-thought-out arguments to make, otherwise you will risk coming across as a lightweight, who doesn't have a confident grip on their supposed area of expertise. If you do have sound arguments, it can be an excellent idea to express them, provided it is done generously and as constructively as possible.

What images should I put online?

Images, as we have discussed, are a powerful way of improving your social media presence. We have discussed profile pictures, so here we will focus on other sorts of images.

First, you need to go back to your brand and consider the image you are trying to project? If you look at a person's images online and the majority show the person at social functions, glass of wine in hand, this will convey certain messages that they may or may not wish for. Similarly, if all of the shots show them in their sports gear, this too will affect their brand. So, when choosing images you need to be conscious as to what you are trying to convey.

Including images of family members is a contentious issue, and there are no hard and fast rules. At the very least, for domestic harmony you should ask the permission of all concerned before posting an image, as you should generally. We think it is important that if family are included it is not exploitative, such as the politician's partner seen standing by the miscreant politician in the fallout of some sex scandal.

If you choose to use images that you have not created, either search for images using Google that are specifically marked as royalty free or public domain. It is not appropriate to simply lift other people's images and pass them off as your own.

Should I create a video about myself?

Videos can be very engaging providing the content is good, and that the video has been well filmed, produced and edited. Videos can be posted to YouTube or Vimeo, or can be incorporated directly into blogs. Depending upon the topic you are blogging on, videos can be very powerful. As a general rule, the shorter the better is the way with videos. Keep them under three minutes if at all possible, unless you are delivering a lecture or similar.

Creating online films and audio with YouTube

Video has never been easier to take or edit. YouTube has become – especially among the under-25s – almost an alternative to television. Consequently, it is not a bad idea to have a presence on YouTube if it is appropriate and consistent with your brand. The key is to produce short, sharp, snappy videos that are well filmed and edited. If you do not have the skills in this area, consider getting outside help. Unfortunately, it is beyond the scope of this book to cover how to produce and edit video.

Assuming you have some good quality footage that is relevant to promoting your brand, upload it to YouTube and provide sharing links to it to promote it. You can promote it simply by sending the link to people or tweeting the link. You can also embed the video in your blogs. There are commands within YouTube that allow you to copy and paste the relevant code into your blog to enable the video to play within your blog.

If you are ever public speaking and the event is being filmed, see if you can ask the organisers for a copy of the footage to allow you to set up your own post.

Creating picture sharing sites with Instagram, Flickr and Pinterest

There are some social media sites that are primarily about images. Three of the most popular are Instagram, Flickr and Pinterest. These sites can be a great place to share photos or other images that are important to you. Again, these images need to be on message in terms of your brand.

What is the point of these sites? Simply it is another way to make contact with other people. If your Instagram photos show you in a good professional light that is on message, your brand is enhanced. In a world where we all carry cameras around with us on our phones, there can be many photo opportunities or 'photo ops'. You could use these sites to share images of meetings, visits or rubbing shoulders with leaders in your industry. It all adds to the brand.

IN A NUTSHELL

We started off this chapter discussing the importance of a brand. What we have tried to reinforce all the way through is that you strengthen your brand by controlling the message. This means giving careful thought to every tweet, comment and blog you put out there. It also means giving careful attention to how you develop your profile on sites such as LinkedIn.

When politicians become ineffective, one of the common reasons is that they have gone 'off message'. They forget the party line on a topic, or forget the topic entirely and go off in unexpected directions that just serve to confuse the general public. The great power of social media is that with a little thought and preparation you can control the message you are putting out there.

7 YOUR FOOTPRINT LINGERS – BE A DILIGENT CURATOR

This chapter will help you to track how you are seen online. It will ask you to think about how you want to be seen and will give you practical tips about how to be seen as professional and highly employable. It will also offer advice about what information prospective employers DO NOT want to see about you online. Finally, it will offer guidance on what to do about those embarrassing photos, titbits of information and unfortunate facts that are out there about you on the internet.

This chapter will cover:

- reviewing how you are seen online
- what information you should have about yourself online
- what information you should not have about yourself online
- dealing with difficult online information.

A window into your life

When you get up in the morning to go to work you may put on a shirt and tie or a smart blouse. You look in the mirror, check that your hair is not too much of a mess and that you haven't got toothpaste around your mouth. You then walk out of the door to work confident in the knowledge that you look great (or, at least, not too bad).

At two o'clock on Saturday morning, on your way back from a night club and munching on a kebab, you probably look a bit less polished. In the middle of a holiday in the sun you might be showing off your tan to your partner or wearing a silly hat. If people at the office saw you they would be so surprised!

It is much more tempting for you or someone else to put pictures of you having fun online than it is to put pictures up of you looking professional in a smart suit. Social media thrives on jokes, glamorous selfies and pictures of you having a laugh.

The problem is that every time someone snaps you in a sombrero and posts it to Instagram, you are leaving a trail of information about yourself online for others to find. Most of this information isn't going to do you any harm (who cares if you wore a silly hat when you were in Spain), but it all contributes to how you are seen by others. Whereas in the past we could keep our sober work selves quite separate from our outrageous weekend selves, increasingly, these two things are coming together.

One response to this is to conclude that you should only present your professional self online and keep everything else off of the web. However, there are lots of good reasons to use social media as part of your social life. This shouldn't be a problem as long as you keep track of how you are seen online, and try and make sure that it is supporting your career aims as well as your social life.

CASE STUDY

Mindy is about to get married and so everyone in the office is talking about stag and hen dos. Joe tells a story about the last stag do that he went on that has everyone laughing. Fred puts Joe's name into Google along with the words 'stag do' and sure enough up pop some pictures of Joe's outrageous antics.

Joe is horrified. It is one thing to do something, but quite another for a permanent record of it to be available on the internet. He retreats back to his office and starts to have a look for information about himself online.

A few Google searches later and he (re)discovers quite a bit about himself.

- *He was the champion of the 1989 under-14s all-Sidcup cross-country run.*
- *He posted some fairly robust opinions about the failings of the Manchester United goalkeeper on the BBC website.*
- *He reviewed the book The Da Vinci Code on Amazon once (he loved it!).*
- *His name, approximate age and the town that he lives in are available for all to see on 192.com.*
- *And then there are those stag do pictures.*

Joe is surprised about how much information is out there about him and disappointed by the focus of this information. He resolves to do something about it.

The first thing that he does is send an email to his friend Rodger asking him to change the privacy settings on the stag do photos. Then he starts putting information about his professional life online. He creates a LinkedIn profile, a blog and a slideshare account and starts posting professionally relevant material. He then creates a Google+ account and uses that to link to all of the professional information about himself. Pretty soon, the online Joe looks very different and much more professional.

How do people see me?

If you want to know how people see you, just go to Google and put your name in: *'Joe Bloggs'*. If you have a common name and nothing comes up, try using a couple of key words: *'Joe Bloggs' Sidcup Marketing*. 'E-stalking' people is usually pretty easy, so it won't take you long before you find yourself.

Have a look and see what comes up. Is it how you want to be seen?

Typically, Google will prioritise a number of things when it displays a search. Google is changing the way that its search works all the time, but, typically, these include:

■ any pages that are owned by Google, e.g. on its social media site Google+
■ any pages that are popular or linked to by lots of other pages
■ Facebook, LinkedIn and Twitter home pages
■ pages where your name (or the search term) are in the heading
■ pages that are on official sites, e.g. government or university sites.

If you do anything online, Google is amazingly good at finding it and making it available for everyone to see.

There are four types of information about you.

Open information	Blind information
The stuff (digital information) that you know and are happy to share with everyone else. E.g. Your LinkedIn profile.	The stuff that everyone else knows about you but you don't know. E.g. A joke that is being shared about how terrible your dress sense is.
Hidden information	**Unknown information**
The stuff that you know but have hidden from everyone else (or maybe just from everyone except your closest friends). E.g. Those pictures of you on a stag do.	The stuff that neither you nor anyone else knows about, but that could still become public. E.g. Some old emails or files that are buried in someone's inbox.

Remember, knowledge is power. You should aim to know about any digital information that is out there about you. Once you know about it you can work out whether you can hide it or whether it should be open.

Should I friend my boss on Facebook?

The internet can bring your professional and personal lives closer together. One way that this can often happen is connecting to your work colleagues on Facebook.

You should always think carefully about who you connect to on Facebook. However, the question of whether you should friend your boss is particularly tricky.

There is no absolute answer. Whether you should friend your boss on Facebook depends on whether you like them, whether you have a relationship outside of the workplace and, above all, on the kind of information that you share on Facebook.

One way that this issue can crop up is if your boss sends you a Facebook friend request. In this case, it can be difficult for you to turn them down without causing offence. Think about whether you want them to have regular access to your Facebook content and whether you want to increase the closeness of your relationship. If you decide to accept them, then make sure you remember that they are there. If you decide not to, you may want to send them an email explaining your decision.

Of course, you can always send your boss a friend request. Again, this will depend on your relationship with them and how comfortable you and they are in linking up beyond work. Again, tread carefully here and be willing to be rejected. Before you send a friend request, it is a good idea to message them and give them the option to turn you down. Everyone uses Facebook in different ways and your boss may not be comfortable sharing his or her information with you. Again, once you are connected on Facebook, DON'T FORGET that they are there.

In general, it is a good idea to take the word 'friend' seriously. If someone isn't your friend in real life, then don't friend them on Facebook.

How can I find out about information that I don't know about?

It is dangerous to have a lot of information about you circulating on the web if you don't know about it. The problem is what can we do about these 'unknown unknowns'?

Three uncomfortable truths

1. It is very likely that there is information available about you somewhere that you don't know about.
2. It is very difficult to track all of this information down and even more difficult to control it all.
3. Most of this information is harmless or banal, but some of it will make your life and career difficult.

It is important to increase your awareness about the information that exists about you online. There are all sorts of things out there that might cause you a problem.

Five types of unknown information that might cause you a problem

1. **Credit rating information.** Companies share information about how risky it would be to lend information to you.
2. **Information held on you by employers.** Especially if this is shared in any way with other employers, e.g. through a reference.
3. **Reviews about your performance as a professional on various rating sites.** For example, you can comment on university lecturers on Rate My Professors (www.ratemyprofessors.com), building professionals on My Builder (www.mybuilder.com) and lawyers on Good Lawyer Guide (www.goodlawyerguide.co.uk).

---

4. **Information about your wider life.** Maybe you are a trainspotter at the weekend. You may not want everyone to know about it, but your club might have posted its membership lists online.
5. **Misinformation and mistaken identity.** People may have posted lies about you either by mistake or maliciously. Also, unless you have a very, very unusual name then someone probably shares your name with you. What if they are in prison or a regular ranter on political discussion boards?

In order to find out what information is out there about you, you will need to be proactive and remain vigilant.

Three tips to find out what is posted about you online

1. Google yourself at least once a month. This will help you to see what Google thinks is the most important information out there about you. BUT BEWARE – Google tries to tailor its search results to what it thinks that you want to see. So it is worth trying to get someone else to Google you as well and see if they get the same results as you.
2. Set up a Google Alert (www.google.co.uk/alerts) based on your name. That way you will see whenever anyone is talking about you online.
3. Join the key social media sites where people might be talking about you. If you are participating, they are less likely to talk about you behind your back (and you are more likely to see when they do).

When do employers look at social media?

The information that is available about you online matters a lot more if employers are looking at it, and if they are choosing to use it as part of recruitment and management processes.

Given the amount of information out there, it would be very surprising if employers never looked at it. We are all curious, and an employer has the added incentive that they are about to commit a large amount of their money or their company's money when they employ you. Even once you have got a job, an employer might consider using social media to keep an eye on what you are doing or to try to understand you better.

Five ways in which employers might use social media

1. **Headhunting.** Some employers use sites such as LinkedIn to source potential candidates for jobs. The development of these sites has brought the cost of headhunting down. Given that conventional recruitment is expensive, the ability to search the web for potential employees is very appealing. If you are going to benefit from this, you will need to have your online CV up to speed.
2. **Recruiting.** During recruitment processes, social media offers employers a wide range of opportunities for finding out further information. This can be used to aid in shortlisting, to help prepare interview questions or to check people out before a job offer is made.
3. **Managing.** Social media offers managers a way to keep an eye on their staff and to better understand them. By using social media you are often opening up the possibility that you will be surveilled by your employer.
4. **Firing.** If a manager or employer is trying to get rid of you or discipline you, then social media offers them a huge potential resource to find incriminating evidence about you.
5. **By chance.** Sometimes, when your managers or employers are using the internet, they might find information about you entirely by chance. You should do your best to make sure that this information is as positive as possible.

Employers' use of social media is rife with problems. It can be time consuming and provide information that is often not relevant to someone's working life. Even more concerning, it raises ethical questions about what is appropriate and what people's reaction would be if they found out that they were being stalked online. We are not advocating these practices, but they clearly do go on so you should make sure that your online footprint supports your career-building.

What would make me look bad online?

The growth of the internet and social media has meant that some of our opinions about privacy have changed. Thirty years ago we would have been horrified if someone took a picture of us in our swimming costume and then mailed it to everyone in the world. However, these days such material is commonly put on Facebook and distributed round our social networks.

Privacy is a very personal thing. We all draw the boundaries in different places and over different images and pieces of information. Some people are happy to share their writing but very cautious about sharing images. For others, it is the other way round. It is important that you spend some time thinking about what information you are happy to share online and what information you would like to avoid being in the public domain.

In the context of our careers, the kind of information that is bad to share is likely to vary with the job. If you work in an avant-garde clothing boutique or record shop, pictures of your tattoos are likely to be a positive advantage. If you work in an accountant's office or a primary school, very daring images might be viewed more negatively. It can be difficult to make absolute predictions about these things, but it is always a good idea to look at what other people in the sector are doing and sharing online before you do it.

In general, most employers are likely to be relaxed about the fact that you have a life outside of work. A single picture of you in fancy-dress outfit or holding a glass of wine is unlikely to do you any great harm. However, there is some merit in there being a balance between professional and social information. If it looks like you just party all of the time then you might find that you aren't taken as seriously as you would like to be.

This is not to say that anything goes. There are a number of things that employers will be really concerned about and that you should do your best to avoid.

Five bits of information that could ruin your career

1. **Examples of unprofessional behaviour** (even when they are jokes). Posting information about how you have cut corners, skived off work, stolen from your employer or cheated your customers is likely to render you unemployable.
2. **Criticising your employer.** We all know that many of our bosses and companies are far from perfect. No one expects you to love going to work every day. But as soon as you start ranting about this online, you cross a line that could endanger your career.
3. **Information about undisclosed criminal activity** (especially where you appear to be celebrating or endorsing this activity). An important sub-set of this is drug use and the celebration of drug-related activities. So, try not to be photographed using a bong!
4. **Excessive drunkenness.** With a few exceptions, no one will mind you having the odd picture of you with a glass of beer or wine. However, if most of your pictures depict your late night adventures in bars then you may appear to have a problem. Even worse are pictures of you clearly drunk and making a fool of yourself.
5. **Bad writing.** Most jobs involve you communicating with other people. Employers are likely to be a lot less positive about you if they see poorly written, poorly spelt and ill-thought-out messages posted by you. In particular the excessive use of text speak is likely to put you on the 'don't hire' pile. k. Do U undRstNd dat. Avoid t% much txt spk o U won't git a job!

How can I deal with difficult and embarrassing material about me online?

As you increase your awareness about what is online, you may find that there are things that you are not happy with. It can be difficult to control online information, but there are various strategies that you can use to manage how you are seen.

Five strategies to deal with potentially damaging information

1. **Don't put it there.** The most effective way to deal with damaging information is to not put it online in the first place. Always ask yourself whether you would be happy for everyone you know and your future employer to see anything before you post it online. If you have any doubts, don't post it!
2. **Delete it or make it more private.** If you have posted something and then come to regret it you may be able to delete it. Most social media sites have an option for you to delete any posts. You cannot guarantee that deleting something will remove it entirely from the public domain, but it will help. Other social media sites allow you to control who can see particular pieces of content. Try to make sure you understand your privacy settings and think about the level of access that you want to offer for each piece of content.
3. **Ask other people to manage the information that they hold on you.** When you can't delete something yourself, you can manage it in other ways. For example, if you find that someone has an embarrassing photo of you on their Facebook account, you can contact them and ask them to remove it or to change the privacy settings. If a public organisation, such as a school or workplace, has posted information about you, you can also ask them to remove it. If they either refuse or don't respond, you may have a legal right to challenge them on this. Many social media sites will take down material that is in dispute while the disputes are ongoing. So, complaining direct to the software provider offers you another way to manage your information.
4. **Swamp it out.** Sometimes there is information that is difficult to get rid of, whatever you do. However, you can try to swamp it out by increasing the volume of positive (or even just boring) information about yourself online. As this material grows it will gradually edge out the embarrassing stuff. Once it is on the second page of Google results, hardly anyone will ever bother to look at it.
5. **Explain it.** Sometimes you can't get rid of something. Perhaps it has been copied and spread around a whole load of different websites. In these cases you might want to create a webpage somewhere that explains the information. For example, this might be a 'I'm not the John Smith who stole the crown jewels' page or a 'Why I stole the crown jewels and am now really sorry' page.

Facebook privacy settings

One of the most common problems that people have with online information is with Facebook privacy settings. Facebook is largely seen as a way to share information with your immediate social circle, but if you aren't careful about your privacy settings it is easy to make information available much more widely.

Facebook has changed the way that its privacy settings work a few times, so you need to keep an eye on the company. At the moment, whenever you post something you can choose one of three main options.

1. Public. Anyone on or off Facebook.
2. Friends. Your friends on Facebook.
3. Only Me.

It is also possible to customise this a bit further so that certain people can or cannot see this content. Facebook's help pages can further assist you with this.

However, this isn't the end of the story. Someone else can take your post and share it with their friends, or even with the whole world. Because of this, it can quickly get passed on to a much wider group of people.

Another thing to be aware of is that Facebook has some core public information that it makes available to everyone regardless of how you set your privacy settings. This public information includes your name, profile picture, cover photo, gender, username, user ID (account number) and networks.

In other words, if something is really private – don't put it on Facebook!

How can I make myself look good online?

We've started this chapter by focusing on damage limitation, but this isn't the whole story. It is important that, as well as trying to minimise the bad stuff, you should also try to maximise the good stuff. The internet gives you a huge opportunity to tell your story, to provide employers with evidence and to show everyone how bright, interesting and employable you are.

Five things that employers want to see about you online

1. **That you are who you say you are.** Employers are most likely to come across your online profile while they have got your CV in their hand. If the two things don't connect you may find that your CV ends up in the bin. Check that the job titles, dates and qualifications that you announce on your CV are not contradicted by any information about you online.
2. **That you can do the job.** At the end of the day, employers are employing you to do a job. Any evidence that exists online that gives them confidence about the work you do is likely to be particularly useful. Examples of your work or testimonials from former employers or clients are all useful ways to demonstrate that you are competent.
3. **That you are enthusiastic.** If an employer finds that you have a great passion for their business or for your chosen profession, that is likely to count in your favour.
4. **That you are knowledgeable.** If you are able to show that you know a lot about the field you work in through creating online content, it is likely to be viewed positively by employers. Maintaining a blog about your chosen field is one easy (if time consuming) way to demonstrate that you are up to date with the latest developments and an expert in your area.
5. **That you are well connected.** Everyone will be impressed if it is clear that you have a large and/or relevant network and that the

---

people in the network think highly of you. This is likely to be even more persuasive if the people in your network are known to the employers you are trying to impress.

Another important thing to remember is that you are not just trying to impress your boss or prospective boss online. Being well respected by your peers and colleagues is very important in helping you to advance in your career. You should think about the content that is available about you online with this in mind.

What if there is nothing about me online?

Using the internet to support your career is difficult. Some people might be tempted to think that it is easier just not to include any information about yourself at all. But, what are the implications of 'going dark' online?

The first problem is ensuring that there is actually nothing about you online. As we have already discussed in this chapter, there is often lots of information about you that you aren't even aware of. All of this material will become more prominent if you don't provide any alternatives.

Even if you are able to turn yourself internet invisible, you may find that it raises questions with employers. Certainly, as you advance in your career, people might ask questions as to why you have made no mark online. The internet provides a record of our lives and achievements, and if you aren't there people might assume that you have never done anything of note.

At the moment, not being online is unlikely to be a major problem (unless you want to work in a field like marketing where digital competence is critical). However, if you aren't online you may find that others who are, and who are using the digital environment creatively, are beating you to some of the opportunities that you are interested in.

IN A NUTSHELL

It is important that you think about how you appear online. You should actively monitor how you are seen and work to try to improve your digital footprint. The first job is to remove the embarrassing and damaging information. The next step is to try to put forward content that actively enhances your career. Employers are paying an increasing amount of attention to your digital footprint and you should make sure that they are going to like what they find.

FINAL THOUGHTS – IF YOU CAN'T BEAT 'EM, YOU'D BETTER JOIN 'EM

Throughout this book we've made the argument that the internet is vital for your career development. Whether you like it or not, the internet isn't about to shrivel up and die! We predict that over the next ten years the internet, in one form or another, is just going to get more and more important for your career. We think that you need to take the plunge and really engage with the potential that it offers you.

If you ignore the internet you will quickly find that the range of jobs that are available to you reduces. You will find it harder to find work, more difficult to build a reputation and may find yourself at the front of the queue when people are being made redundant.

On the other hand, if you grab the opportunities that the internet offers to you, your career should go from strength to strength. Effective users of the internet hear about job opportunities, have better networks, are better known and are more able to be effective at work. The internet can help you make the most of yourself and promote it to others.

Of course, it is possible to use the internet badly. Your future career can be damaged if you spray badly spelt, idiotic abuse all over the internet. Even bad jokes or overly sharing your crazy nights out could have a negative effect if you are not careful. So, always think carefully about how others might see you.

In summary, the internet offers you great career power. But, with great career power comes great career responsibility. That is why we wrote this book. We hope that it has been useful for you. We have argued that if you pay attention to our seven golden rules you will be able to use the internet to make great strides in your career.

Remember the golden rules:

1. **Change is inevitable – be an adventurous explorer!** Remember that fortune favours the brave and that in a fast-changing environment like the internet you need to be fleet of foot. Be positive about learning new things and willing to be flexible. Above all, remember planmanship and RAPID-CPR (Revise, Abandon, Pause, Implement, Devise, Copy, Promote and Revive)!

2. **Information is power – collect as much as you can!** The internet puts the world at your fingertips, but you have to be clever to avoid being buried under information overload. Effective career-builders will make use of a wide range of information sources and learn how to search effectively, make use of alerts and use their network to help them find really useful information.

3. **The internet is a jungle – be a critical thinker!** The internet is full of all sorts of information: good, bad and ugly. If you are going to make the most of this vast library you need to be good at sorting the wheat from the chaff. We suggest that you subject everything to the CRAAP test (Currency, Relevance, Authority, Accuracy And Purpose). Don't get fooled again!

4. **Networks are vital – be an effective connector!** Your career is built one relationship at a time. The more people you know and the better you are at staying in touch with them, the more help you can call on with your career. At the heart of effective networking is remembering that helping others is just as important as asking for help. And at the heart of effective online networking is remembering that this is a real relationship, even if it is taking place through a computer.

5. **Interaction is important – be a perceptive communicator!** Talking to people is really important. Every time you send someone anything, from a tweet to a nine-screen email, you are telling them something about you, your career and what you are like. Most employers rate your communication skills as a pretty important aspect of your employability. Make sure that you provide lots of good evidence that you are clear, concise and considerate.

6. **Build a brand – be a skilled storyteller!** Everything you post about yourself tells a story. Your colleagues and your prospective employers will be trying to piece this story together and work out whether they like it. If you want your story to have a happy ending, then try to make sure that you tell it well. Effective career storytelling is all about thinking about how you want others to see you and doing your best to build up the right evidence.

7. **Your footprint lingers – be a diligent curator!** You will be amazed at all of the information that is out there on the internet about you. Even if you are a Facebook refusenik or a cave-dwelling hermit, it is likely that someone has posted something about you somewhere. If not, people might wonder where you've been all your life. To ensure that your digital footprint is helping your career, you should be aware of what it contains. So, research yourself and think carefully about the story that you are telling.

If you follow these seven rules you should see your career take off. As we've argued throughout the book, you need to be active online and offline. A brilliant online profile is a great start, but you will also need to network and build relationships face to face. There is no such thing as an 'online career', but there is increasingly no such thing as an 'offline career' either. You have one career and you might as well use all of the tools, online and offline, to make it the best one possible.

We wish you luck in your career! May the force be with you, may all the odds be in your favour and don't let the internet trolls, skateboarding kittens and celebrity banalities grind you down. The internet offers you a chance to change your life for the better; we hope that you grasp it!

INTERNET-TO-ENGLISH DICTIONARY

@ – meaning 'at', a form of address particularly in Twitter, e.g. @Pigironjoe, @DrJimBright or @DavidAWinter are the authors' Twitter addresses. The term is also used when somebody wants to refer specifically to another person in a 'thread' (see below). The '@' symbol when used in some social media sites is a command and the site will interpret whatever follows it as a person's address. When this happens, the other person is alerted that they are being referred to in a post – see 'Mention' below.

Button – a graphic that appears on the screen on a social media page which, when pressed (i.e. mouse pointer moved over and mouse clicked), navigates the user to another part of the social media site.

Emoticons – small visual symbols that are used to convey emotion or meaning, e.g. ☺. These are often made up of combinations of ordinary keyboard characters e.g. ;->.

Flames, flaming and flame wars – online arguments that serve little purpose and can often turn personal or nasty.

Follower – a person who connects to your social media account and receives notifications every time you post something or alter your social media profile – especially in Twitter and LinkedIn.

Friend – used as a verb and noun. A friend is a person you have invited to link with you or someone whose invitation you have accepted. The act of inviting a friend is 'friending'. The opposite – 'unfriending' – is when you remove a person from a list of your contacts.

Hashtag or '#' – stands for a label, usually referring to a discussion thread or a person or event that others can use to search for related information. For instance, 'Benny Hill appears with Irene Handl #ItalianJob' could be a tweet in a series of tweets discussing the film *The Italian Job*. Others who search for #ItalianJob would be able to find this and other similar messages on this topic. See also 'Tagging'.

Haters – people who express hatred for someone (usually a public figure) online. Online hate speech can often be violent and disturbing.

Like – pressing a button that sends a message to another person's social media profile indicating your appreciation or approval of their post.

Mention – specifically referring to another person by including their social media title in a post. For example, the tweet 'as @IreneHandl argued, doing that gives cats ideas and should be avoided' includes a mention for user Irene Handl.

Netiquette – the rules and conventions that govern online behaviour. They are rarely written down and need to be absorbed by watching and reflecting on the behaviours of others.

Newbie or nOOb – someone unfamiliar with the conventions of a particular internet forum.

Post/Update/Tweet – a message, news or other information that you have submitted to social media.

Profile – your personal information that is publicly available on your social media site. It may include a photograph and biographical information which could be minimal (e.g. Twitter) or extensive and CV-like (e.g. LinkedIn).

Really Simple Syndication (RSS) – technology that allows you to subscribe to a range of news feeds and to read them through an RSS reader (available from most app stores).

Selfie – a picture taken of yourself using a handheld device such as a mobile phone.

Share – forwarding somebody else's post to all of your followers; this may include 'retweeting' another person's tweet on Twitter.

Tagging – associating information, particularly photographs (especially in Facebook), with a social media user. So, if somebody posts a photograph of you and your colleagues at the company spring conference, another user may 'tag' you – i.e. enter your social media name to caption either the whole of the photograph or your face. When this happens, you receive a notification that you have been 'tagged' in the photograph by such and such a user.

Thread – a discussion on a specific topic with contributions from several or many different users. Discussion threads often have a hashtag (see above) associated with them to help people find the thread and all the contributions. Contributors are encouraged to include the hashtag when posting. This is particularly helpful in Twitter discussions that otherwise have no way of organising information into threads.

TLAs or Three Letter Acronyms – shortenings used in online and mobile communication. Many of them have more than three letters!

Trending – social media sites collect statistics about particularly popular discussion threads. In particular, Facebook and Twitter promote the top trending discussions or topics. This can be useful if you want to follow fast changing news stories as they happen, such as revolutions in countries or whatever Kim Kardashian is doing today.

Trolls – people who seek to attract attention by making provocative comments. A troll is someone who disagrees or argues with you for no reason.

ENDNOTES

i. These principles are based on the seven Cs of digital career literacy, which were first published in Hooley, T. (2012). 'How the internet changed career: framing the relationship between career development and online technologies'. *Journal of the National Institute for Career Education and Counselling (NICEC)* 29 (Oct. 2012).

ii. Pryor, R. and Bright, J. (2011). *The Chaos Theory of Careers*. Abingdon: Routledge.

iii. Ipsos (2013). 'Socialogue: The Most Common Butterfly On Earth Is The Social Butterfly'. Retrieved from www.ipsos-na.com/news-polls/ pressrelease.aspx?id=5954. Accessed 26 February 2016.

iv. Hamrick K. (2011). 'How much time do Americans spend eating each day?' Retrieved from http://blogs.usda.gov/2011/11/22/how-much-time- do-americans-spend-eating. Accessed 26 February 2016.

v. Wilson, C. (2009). 'Will My Video Get 1 Million Views on YouTube?' Retrieved from www.slate.com/articles/technology/webhead/2009/07/will_ my_video_get_1_million_views_on_youtube.html. Accessed 26 February 2016.

vi. Hooley, T., Hutchinson, J. and Watts, A. G. (2010). *Enhancing Choice? The Role of Technology in the Career Support Market*. London: UKCES.

vii. Granovetter, M. (1973). 'The strength of weak ties'. *American Journal of Sociology* 78(6): 1360–80.

viii. Sense about Science (2010). 'Making Sense of Statistics'. Retrieved from www.senseaboutscience.org/resources.php/1/making-sense-of-statistics. Accessed 26 February 2016.

ix. Bolton, Paul (2010). 'How to spot spin and inappropriate use of statistics'. House of Commons Library briefing paper: SN04446. Retrieved from http://researchbriefings.parliament.uk/ResearchBriefing/Summary/ SN04446. Accessed 10 March 20156.

x. Meriam Library, California State University (2010). 'Evaluating Information – Applying the CRAAP Test'. Retrieved from www.csuchico.edu/lins/ handouts/eval_websites.pdf. Accessed 26 February 2016.

xi. Putnam, R. (2000). *Bowling Alone: The Collapse and Revival of American Community*. New York: Simon & Schuster.

xii. Iyengar, S. (2010). *The Art of Choosing*. London: Hachette Digital.

xiii. Vallacher, R.R., Wegner, D.M. and Frederick, J. (1987). 'The presentation of self through action identification'. *Social Cognition* 5: 301–22.

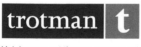

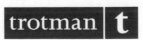

PASS WITH FLYING COLOURS

ORIGINAL TESTS PLUS EXPERT TIPS

CERI RODERICK & JAMES MEACHIN

Find out how to:

- Become a savvy test taker

- Boost your confidence and improve performance

- Stand out from the other candidates

Order today from www.trotman.co.uk